JOSE MOURII
REAL MADRID
A TACTICAL ANALYSIS
ATTACKING

WRITTEN BY ATHANASIOS TERZIS

PUBLISHED BY

Jose Mourinho's Real Madrid
A Tactical Analysis - Attacking

First Published October 2012 by SoccerTutor.com

Info@soccertutor.com | www.SoccerTutor.com

UK: 0208 1234 007 | **US:** (305) 767 4443 | **ROTW:** +44 208 1234 007
ISBN 978-0-9566752-7-9

Author
Athanasios Terzis © 2012

Translation from Greek to English:
Chatzimanoli Eleni

Reviewing the manuscript:
Chatzimanoli Eleni

Edited by
Alex Fitzgerald - SoccerTutor.com

Cover Design by
Alex Macrides, Think Out Of The Box Ltd.
email: design@thinkootb.com Tel: +44 (0) 208 144 3550

Diagrams
Diagram designs by SoccerTutor.com. All the diagrams in this book have been created
using SoccerTutor.com Tactics Manager Software available from **www.SoccerTutor.com**

Note: While every effort has been made to ensure the technical accuracy of the content
of this book, neither the author nor publishers can accept any responsibility for any
injury or loss sustained as a result of the use of this material.

ABOUT THE AUTHOR

ATHANASIOS TERZIS

- UEFA B coaching licence
- M.S.C. certification in coaching and conditioning.

I played soccer for several teams in the third and fourth Greek division. At the age of 29 I stopped playing and focused on studying football coaching. Since then I have been the head coach of several semi-pro football teams in Greece and worked as a technical director in the Academies of DOXA Dramas (Greek football league, second division).

I wrote and published two books - '4-3-3 the application of the system' and '4-4-2 with diamond in midfield, the application of the system.' I decided to proceed in something more specific so coaches would have an idea of how top teams apply the same systems. My third book, 'FC Barcelona, A Tactical Analysis' has sold thousands across the world and has had a great reception from fellow coaches, impressed at the level of detail in the blueprint of Guardiola's team. My next project was always going to be Mourinho's Real Madrid and I strongly believed they would win the league, so I decided to study them for the 2011-12 season.

Analysing games tactically is a great love and strength of mine. I think teams have success only when they prepare well tactically.

I have always been interested to watch Real Madrid's games in the past, as well as many of Jose Mourinho's past teams. I have analysed Real Madrid's

tactics during the 2011-12 season which helped Mourinho create a title winning side to I watched every Real Madrid game in the 2011-12 season creating a set of highly detailed notes on each.

I watched many of the matches over 20 times. The matches were separated according to the opposing team's formation. This book is made up of over a 1000 hours of extensive research and analysis of Jose Mourinho's side.

There were many key tactics, but Real were particularly good in the transition phase and were renowned as the best counter attacking team in Europe.

Other key features of Real's successful season were their improved ability at winning the ball back immediately, a direct style which aimed to create chances after 3 or 4 passes, long balls to the forwards, avoiding 'risky' passes in crucial areas and maintaining cohesion during the attacking phase to prepare for potential negative transitions.

Real Madrid may not have had the style and possession of Barcelona (their closest rivals), but Mourinho's tactics which are set out in this book enabled Real to comfortably beat them to the La Liga title.

Athanasios Terzis

TO MELINA AND ELEFTHERIA...

TACTICAL ANALYSIS FORMAT

1. Outline of the tactical phase of play

2. Progressions within the phase of play

3. Diagrams to support the positions and movements of the players

4. Assessment of the phase of play

KEY

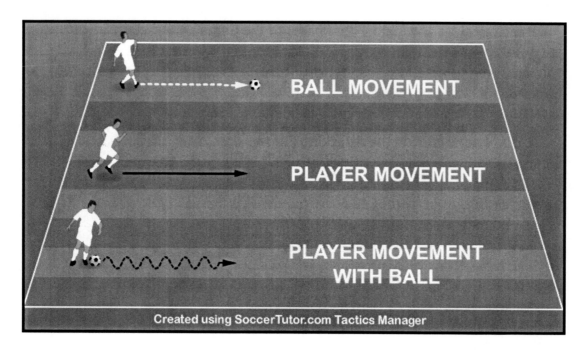

BALL MOVEMENT

PLAYER MOVEMENT

PLAYER MOVEMENT WITH BALL

Created using SoccerTutor.com Tactics Manager

CONTENTS

HOW THE PHASES OF PLAY WERE PRODUCED FOR THIS BOOK

Terzis Athanasios has a great skill of analysing games tactically and watched every Real Madrid game during the 2011-12 season. This book is made up of over 1000 hours of extensive research and analysis of Jose Mourinho's side.

The Steps of Research and Analysis

1. Terzis watched the games, observing Real Madrid's patterns of play and making notes.

2. Once the same phase of play occurred a number of times (at least 10) the tactics would be decoded and more detailed notes were written down, often separated according to the opposing team's formation.

3. The positioning of each player on the pitch is studied in great detail, including their body shape.

4. Each individual movement with or without the ball is also recorded in detail.

5. Once all conceivable phases of play had been studied and analysed, SoccerTutor.com's Tactics Manager software was used to create all the diagrams in this book.

6. Finally, the key aspects of Real Madrid's tactics were assessed and are explained clearly with notes and detailed descriptions.

HOW TO USE USE THIS CONTENT IN YOUR PRACTICES AND SESSIONS

Some coaches may ask 'How do I use these phases of play to create practices and sessions?'

Here we are going to show you how.

We are going to use a phase of play shown below from Chapter 5. This is a phase of play which was repeated many times by Real Madrid in the 2011-12 season.

FULL BACK'S OVERLAPPING RUN ON THE LEFT FLANK

On diagram 24.12, Ronaldo receives the long ball from Pepe wide on the left.

Ronaldo receives and moves towards the centre as Marcelo makes an overlapping run. Higuain drops deep to receive unmarked inside. No.4 had to drop back to cover No.2's position to prevent a 2v1 situation on the flank. Ronaldo decides to pass the ball to Higuain.

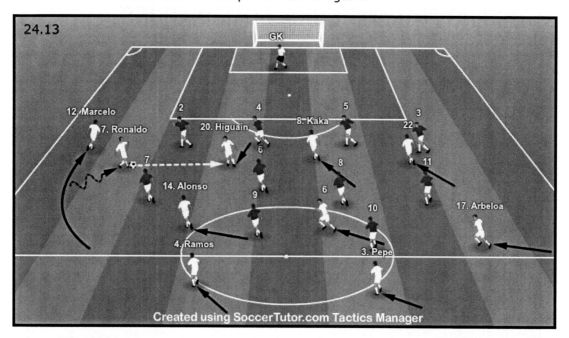

Higuain moves forward with the ball and has 3 passing options. Alonso again provides safety, covering for Marcelo's forward run.

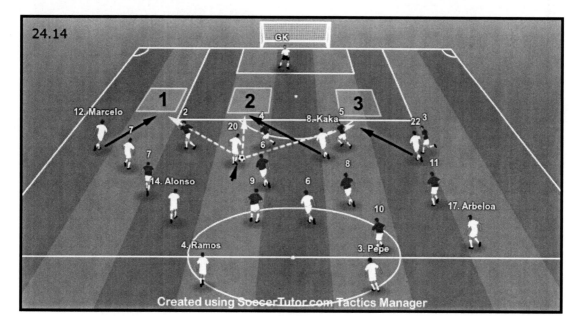

EXAMPLE PRACTICE

SWITCHING PLAY AND QUICK COMBINATIONS

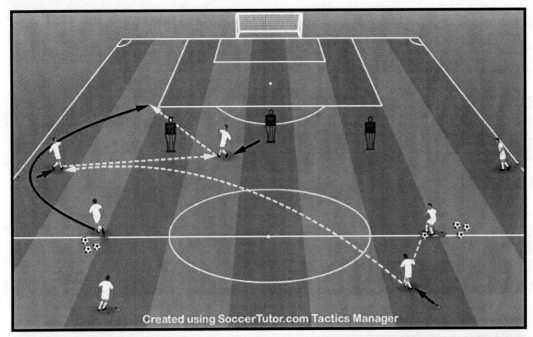

Created using SoccerTutor.com Tactics Manager

Objective

To develop switching play and quick combinations.

Description

Using a 2 thirds of a pitch, 7 players practice this passing sequence.

6 players are positioned on the cones as shown, with the seventh positioned next to the middle mannequin.

The players play the passes as shown on one side with the sequence ending with the overlapping full back. Alternate the side the combination is played. Change the roles often.

Coaching Points

1. The passing needs to be highly accurate and well timed with the correct angles used.

2. Players should check away from the cones or mannequin to create space.

3. The speed of play needs to be high to switch play effectively, so the use of 1 touch when possible can be key.

4. The full back's run from deep needs to be well timed to meet the final pass at pace.

PRACTICE PROGRESSION

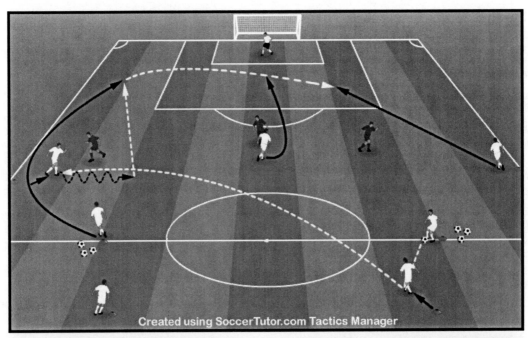

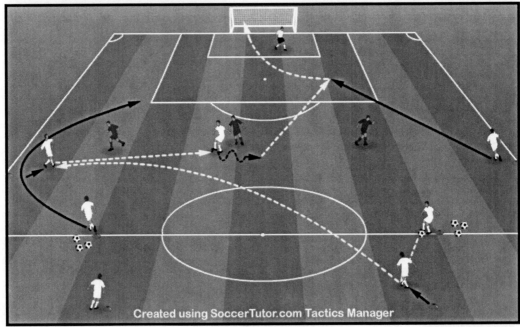

Objective

To develop switching play and quick combination play.

Description

Using a 2 thirds of a pitch, 7 attacking players, 3 defenders and 1 goalkeeper are involved in this practice. The defenders have been added to progress the exercise. The winger on the opposite side is also now involved to add to the attacking options.

6 players are positioned on the cones as shown with the other man in a forward's position.

The drill starts off the same way, with a switch of play to the flank. The full back makes an overlapping run, but this time the forward has the freedom to make the decision for the final ball. 2 example combinations are shown.

Coaching Points

1. Encourage the players to be inventive, using a different combination each time.

2. Players should check away from their markers to create space.

3. The quality of movement is key and you should monitor correct body shape, timing of runs and the angle/ direction of the pass.

4. Add 1 more defender once the players are comfortable with the practice.

INTRODUCTION

Jose Mourinho took charge of Real Madrid for the beginning of the 2010-11 season. During this season Real Madrid only managed to win the Copa del Ray. In this book we analyse his second season in charge in which he won the 2011-12 La Liga title.

Mourinho has always been more successful in his second season with every club he has managed. During his second season in Porto he won the Champions League title as well as the Portuguese Championship. At Chelsea he managed to win the Premier League title, the F.A. cup and reach the quarter finals of the Champions League. In his second season. With Inter Milan, he led his team to the treble in his second season, winning the Scudetto, the Italian cup and the Champions League. During his second season with Madrid (2011-12) they managed to win the title against Guardiola's Barcelona as they finished first in La Liga.

Mourinho has used several formations during his career as a coach. At Porto, he mainly used the 4-4-2 with a diamond in midfield. At Chelsea he used the 4-3-3 formation and the diamond 4-4-2. During his time at Inter he mainly used the 4-2-3-1 and only in some matches he used the diamond 4-4-2 formation. At Real Madrid he chose to use the 4-2-3-1 formation and Moruinho signed players that fitted into this particular formation.

This book set focuses on studying how Real Madrid applied the 4-2-3-1 formation in each phase of the game under the guidance of one of the most successful coaches in the recent history of football.

This book was written after analysing all of Real Madrid 's matches during the 2011-2012 season. Highly detailed notes on every match were written down and were separated according to the opposition's formation.

During this season Real Madrid proved to be a very effective team during both the defending and attacking phase. Their transitions were really fantastic, as they relied a lot on their counter attacking ability, especially when the opposition played high up the pitch.

Real Madrid vastly improved their ability to win the ball back. They often succeeded in winning the ball back immediately after losing it. This way of carrying out the negative transition helped the team to dominate their games in both La Liga and the Champions League.

Specifically during the attacking phase, Real used a more direct style of play seeking to create chances after completing only a couple of passes (3 or 4) or by using long balls directed to the forwards rather than maintaining possession while searching for the opposition's weaknesses.

When building up from the back, the defenders did not use risky passes towards the midfielders if they were under pressure from the opposition. They preferred a safer way of building up play. They made long passes towards Benzema or Ronaldo to avoid losing possession in crucial areas.

Real Madrid's forwards (and Ozil) were very capable in creating and exploiting free space, especially down the flanks. The left footed Di Maria and the right footed Ronaldo used to attack on the on the right and the left side respectively. So they tended to converge towards the inside in order to search for the final pass or a shoot on goal from outside the box. These two players (especially Di Maria) used to use in swinging crosses from the edge of the penalty area, whereas the full backs moved to advanced positions in order to use out swinging crosses for the Madrid forwards who were very capable at winning aerial duels.

The team retained its balance and cohesion at all times during attacking the attacking phase. This resulted in the immediate regaining of possession and led the team to attack again and again.

The key player was Alonso who was a very good reader of the tactical situations and took up the appropriate positions in the different situations. This allowed Real to win the ball back immediately.

In the defensive phase, Alonso was again the key man as Ronaldo to do very little defensive duties. So Real's holding midfielder had to recognise the tactical situation and provide help to Marcelo and prevent the opposition from outnumbering them on the left.

The team usually pressed high up the pitch to win the ball back immediately. The way the pressing was carried out had a lot to do with the wingers' positioning (balanced or goal sided).

During the positive transition, the team was very effective. Ronaldo's poor defensive position became a weapon for Mourinho during this phase.

The pace of Ronaldo, Benzema and Di Maria, together with Ozil's passing skills made Real Madrid the best counter attacking team in Europe.

CHAPTER 1

THE CHARACTERISTICS OF REAL MADRID PLAYERS

THE CHARACTERISTICS OF REAL MADRID PLAYERS

All the Real Madrid players are international, top class players. Some of them are very flexible. Ramos, Diarra, Coentrao, Ozil and Benzema were all used in more than one position during the 2011-2012 season.

There were some players who were used in almost all of the matches of the season. These players were Casillas, Alonso and Ronaldo.

Unlike Barcelona, Real Madrid did not produce players from its own youth system, with the exception of Casillas, so the team had to spend a large amount of money to buy these players. That is why Real Madrid is said to be the most expensive team in the world.

THE PLAYERS

GOALKEEPER: IKER CASILLAS

Casillas is a Spanish international and one of the top European goalkeepers of the last decade. He is more of a reaction goalkeeper as he did very well in blocking shots. However, he is also capable of closing down one on ones quickly effectively. He also has good technical skills in receiving and passing the ball which enabled him to take part in the team's build-up play whenever it was necessary.

RIGHT BACK: ALVARO ARBELOA

Arbeloa is also a Spanish international. He was a very reliable player as regards to his defensive duties. He was capable of defending both on the ground and in the air with great success. During the attacking phase he created width down the right flank when Di Maria took up a position towards the centre and tried to exploit the free space by using mainly inside and overlapping runs, when the man in possession (mainly Di Maria) had a wide position.

Arbeloa did not contribute as much as the other full back Marcelo did during the attacking phase. Real Madrid's right back had very quick reactions during the negative transition by applying pressure immediately or by taking up the appropriate positions in order for the team to regain possession quickly. Mourinho also used Diarra and Ramos in this position.

LEFT BACK: MARCELO

Marcelo is a Brazilian international and is a very skilful and fast player. He had a great contribution during the attacking phase. He worked in collaboration with Ronaldo and most of the time he was the one who created width on the left, as the Portuguese used to play more centrally. Marcelo also used to make driving runs with the ball towards the centre or inside runs in order to receive the ball. He would look to move into the available space behind the defence every time the ball carrier (Ronaldo, Ozil or the centre forward) took up a wide position on the left.

The Brazilian was not as effective when he had to carry out his defensive duties. That is why Coentrao took up the role of the left back when Mourinho wanted a more reliable defensive player.

RIGHT CENTRAL DEFENDER: PEPE

The Portuguese international is a very tough player. He and Ramos formed a partnership which had great ability in winning one on ones duels and defending high crosses. Pepe was very dominant in the air and is very fast. However, when he had to defend on the ground he would not hesitate to cross the line frequently by committing careless and clumsy tackles. He was not technically skilled and did not contribute much in the build up, especially when under pressure. R. Albiol and Varane were the two players also used in the same position when Pepe was not available.

LEFT CENTRAL DEFENDER: SERGIO RAMOS

Ramos is also a Spanish international. He is physically strong and fast just like Pepe, but he is far more skilful. Ramos was previously used as a right back. Mourinho did the same in some matches during the 2011-12 season. Due to his technical ability, he contributed more during the team's attacking play than Pepe by passing and moving forward with the ball.

He also scored a few goals, mainly headers from crosses from set pieces. Carvalho replaced Ramos in several matches.

LEFT DEFENSIVE MIDFIELDER: ALONSO

He was the key link player for Real. He held the role of the holding midfielder. He was mainly used on the left, where Marcelo and Ronaldo were attacking minded players, so he had to provide cover for their forward runs always being the safety player. He was very strong at winning duels and very capable of reading the tactical situation arising on the field. He used to take up the appropriate positions in order to deal with any potential problems.

During the defensive phase, he filled every gap that was created in the defensive line caused by the extensive shift of the central defenders and he used to create superiority in numbers around the ball zone in order for the regaining of

possession to be easier for the team. As a result of this, he finished the season having made 426 interceptions/ tackles in all competitions during the 2011-12 season. Alonso kept the team balanced when Ronaldo used to take up a defensive position between the full back and the central defender.

During the attacking phase Alonso was the link player between the defenders and the forwards. He had a high level of passing accuracy using short and long passes towards the weak side of the opposing team. Alonso's great contribution was during the negative transitions, as he always took up intelligent positions which enabled him to apply immediately pressure on the ball and helped his team to regain possession quickly. Sahin was Alonso's back up, but he only played in a few matches as Mourinho relied on Alonso who started in almost every match.

RIGHT DEFENSIVE MIDFIELDER: SAMI KHEDIRA.

He is physically very strong as a player with high levels of stamina. He contributed a lot during the attacking phase. Khedira used to make a lot of runs behind the opposition's full back to taking advantage of the free space when the ball was in Di Maria's possession down the flank. He frequently entered the opposing team's penalty area to receive potential crosses from the wingers or the full backs and scored 4 goals during the 2011-12 season.

During the defensive phase Khedira participated effectively in the collective pressing. He was very capable of winning one on ones having 195 interceptions/ tackles in all competitions during the 2011-12 season and helped Real to dominate in midfield. Diarra replaced Khedira in several matches. Diarra was a very reliable player in his defensive duties but he was not as effective during the attacking phase. Mourinho also used Granero as a defensive midfielder, a more balanced player who was able to contribute equally in all of the phases of the match.

ATTACKING MIDFIELDER: MESUT OZIL

The German is a very talented player with great technical skills. His first touch is first class and his killer passes frequently put the forwards into shooting positions close to the opposition's goal.

During the attacking phase he worked in collaboration with Ronaldo and Benzema mainly. Several times during the matches Ozil took advantage of the available space on the left, often created by Ronaldo dropping deeper.

During the defensive phase as an attacking midfielder, Ozil used to take up the appropriate defensive positions in order for the pressing to be successful. This was despite not being the type of player who would work hard when he was involved in duels.

When Ozil played as a right forward, his defensive positioning was rather poor. He used to take up a defensive position between the central defender and the full back and rarely tracked the forward runs of his direct opponent. He scored 6 goals and had 23 assists during the 2011-12 season. Mourinho used Kaka as an attacking midfielder when Ozil was not available or when he was moved to play as a right winger.

LEFT FORWARD: CRISTIANO RONALDO

He was the star of this team. Ronaldo has been one of the top European players during the last 8 years. He won the FIFA World Player of the Year award in 2008. The Portuguese international has been the team's top goal scorer in each season since he signed for Real Madrid. During the 2011-2012 season he scored 59 goals in all competitions. He displayed outstanding technique, pace and explosiveness which made him almost unstoppable in one on ones against opposition defenders. He not only has remarkable shooting ability but also with heading. Despite being right footed, Ronaldo was used as a left winger.

During the attacking phase, when Real Madrid used a gradual build up he used to take up positions towards the centre which enabled him to find more shooting opportunities. This positioning close to the centre gave him more chances to enter the opposition's penalty area to receive killer passes from Di Maria or Ozil, as well as crosses from Di Maria or Arbeloa on the right and Marcelo or Ozil on the left.

When Real used fast counter attacks Ronaldo found more space on the flanks to take advantage of his pace.

During the defensive phase he did not have a significant contribution as his positioning was rather poor.

RIGHT FORWARD:
ANGEL DI MARIA

The Argentine international is a very hard worker and is always full of energy. He has good technical skills, pace with or without the ball and great explosiveness.

During the attacking phase, he frequently made driving runs from the right towards the centre using his preferred left foot. These runs ended up with a shot towards the goal or a final vertical or diagonal pass towards Benzema, Higuain or Ronaldo. When he was positioned on the flank he would get in swinging crosses into the box, which were accurate and created goal scoring opportunities. Di Maria provided 15 assists and scored 7 goals in all competitions during the 2011-12 season.

In the defensive phase, Di Maria participated very well in the collective pressing and tracked the forward runs of the opposition's left back. He also had a great contribution with extremely quick reactions when Madrid had lost possession. Callejon was often brought on to replace Di Maria. The youngster participated effectively in the team's defensive play but he did not have the quality of Di Maria in order to be as effective in the attacking phase.

CENTRE FORWARD:
BENZEMA / HIGUAIN

Benzema and Higuain are both top class players. Both of them were used in the centre forward position throughout the season.

Higuain has the features of a typical centre forward and liked to play close to the penalty area. Benzema is more comfortable in all areas of the pitch, even when playing down the flanks. They both have great technical qualities as well as the killer instinct in front of goal.

Benzema scored 31 goals in all competitions during the 2011-2012 season and Higuain scored 26.

Mourinho managed to get them involved in the team's defensive phase as well as in the negative transitions during which they both worked hard in order for the team to regain possession.

JOSE MOURINHO

PLAYER

- Rio Ave, 1980 - 1982
- Belenenses, 1982 - 1983
- Sesimbra, 1983 - 1985
- Comercio E Insustria, 1985 - 1987

MANAGER

Benfica (2000)

Uniao de Leiria (2001 - 2002)

Porto (2002 - 2004)

- Uefa Champions League 2003-04
- Primeira Liga 2002-03, 2003-04
- Uefa Cup 2002-03
- Taça de Portugal, 2002-03
- Supertaça Cândido de Oliveira, 2003

Chelsea (2004-07)

- Premier League 2004-05, 2005-06
- FA Cup 2006-07
- League Cup, 2004-05, 2006-07

Inter Milan (2008-10)

- Uefa Champions League 2009-10
- Serie A, 2008-09, 2009-10
- Coppa Italia, 2009-10
- Supercoppa Italiana, 2008

Real Madrid (2010 - present)

- La Liga, 2011-2012
- Copa Del Ray, 2010-2011

Mourinho is one of the best coaches in recent history. He started his career at Benfica and then Uniao Leiria. In January 2002 he took charge of Porto where he had two unbelievable seasons. He won the Portuguese league title twice, as well as the Portuguese cup and two European Cups, the UEFA cup in 2003 and the Champions League in 2004.

This success led Roman Abramovich to sign him as the head coach of Chelsea, who were becoming one of the most promising sides in Europe. Mourinho was in charge of Chelsea for 3 seasons and he managed to win 2 consecutive Premier League titles (2005 and 2006).

In the beginning of his fourth season at Chelsea he was forced to resign. For the 2008-09 season Mourinho moved to Inter Milan where he had 2 very successful years (2008-2010).

Success was again achieved by the Portuguese as he won the Scudetto during his first season and the treble (Scudetto, Coppa Italia and the Champions League) during his second year.

The following season, the chairman of Real Madrid Florentino Perez signed Mourinho to lead Real back to the top of the Spanish League. Mourinho's first season in Madrid was not that successful as he only managed to win the Copa Del Rey. However, he again achieved success in his second season as the team won the La Liga title ahead of Guardiola's Barcelona side.

Mourinho has been more successful during his second season at every team he has taken charge of.

REAL MADRID'S FIRST 11

FOR THE 2011-12 SEASON (4-2-3-1 FORMATION)

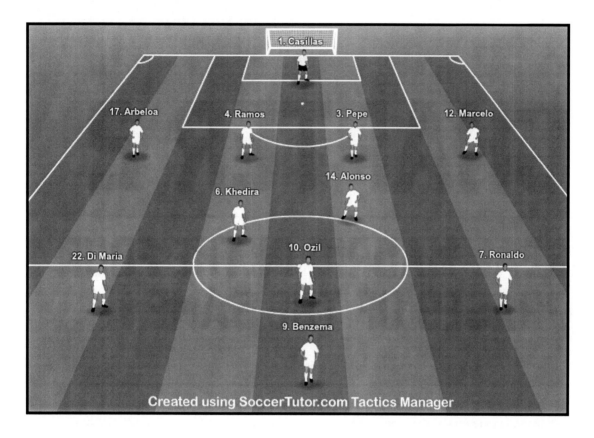

CHAPTER 2

REAL MADRID IN THE FOUR PHASES OF THE GAME

REAL MADRID IN THE DEFENSIVE PHASE

When Real Madrid were not in possession, the players mainly applied pressure near the opposition's penalty area to regain the ball. The defenders applied aggressive zonal marking in collaboration with the midfielders and the forwards. This would deny time and space for their direct opponents.

The midfielders took up intelligent positions during the defensive phase in order to double mark the opposing players. The aim was to regain possession back as quickly as possible and to have high percentages of possession during the games, dominating the opposition.

REAL MADRID IN THE TRANSITION FROM ATTACK TO DEFENCE

Mourinho created a very effective team during the transition phase.

For the negative phase, the Real Madrid players prepared well when the team's attacking phase was in process. The players made sure they retained the team's balance for every single second when attacking the opposition.

When Real Madrid lost possession there was always a safety player close to the play who could put pressure on the ball straight away. Importantly, the reactions of the players around the ball zone were immediate and they all worked very hard to regain possession quickly.

When the immediate regaining of possession was not possible, the players made sure they secured the central zone and forced the ball wide. The effectiveness of Real Madrid during the negative transitions meant the team could dominate games and dictate the rhythm in almost every match.

REAL MADRID IN THE ATTACKING PHASE

When Real Madrid had possession the team tried to create width. This width was created on the left through the advanced positioning near the side line of Marcelo, while on the right either Di Maria stayed wide or Arbeloa moved into a wide advanced position when Di Maria was positioned towards the centre.

The Real Madrid players were very comfortable attacking down the flanks or through the centre. When the team created superiority in numbers in the central zone with Ronaldo and Di Maria moving into this area, the players mainly used short vertical and diagonal passes.

If the opposition tried to restrict the available space by moving their wide midfielders towards the centre, Real's defensive midfielders or the central defenders used long passes towards the full backs who stayed in wide positions.

Alonso was the player who dictated the rhythm of the game and helped the team move from the second to the third stage of the build up play. The final passes (third stage of the build up) were usually made by Ozil from the central zone or by Di Maria and Ronaldo who were very comfortable in driving the ball towards the centre. These runs usually ended with an assist (vertical or diagonal) towards the players who timed a run into the box.

Real Madrid forwards were tall and very effective in winning headers in the box. So when the team tried to build up play down the flanks, the attacking moves often ended with a high out swinging cross. These crosses were mainly Marcelo's and sometimes Ozil's from the left and Arbeloa's on the right.

Khedira also used to get into crossing positions on the right, but his crosses were usually made from the edge of the penalty area on the right and were rather low.

Di Maria mainly and sometimes Ozil on the right and Ronaldo on the left used to use in swinging crosses from wide positions outside the penalty area.

REAL MADRID IN THE TRANSITION FROM DEFENCE TO ATTACK

As mentioned before, Real Madrid were very effective in the transition phase. During the positive transitions they were seen as the best team in the world for the 2011-2012 season.

The success in this phase resulted from the players' particular abilities. With the blend of Ronaldo, Di Maria, Benzema and Higuain's pace, Ozil was very capable of making the perfect pass at the right time for them to run onto.

Mourinho used Ronaldo's poor defensive positioning (as he stayed high up the field during the defensive phase) as one of his main weapons for fast breaks.

Real even had the capability to use the situation of defending a set piece as an opportunity to play on the break and create goal scoring chances.

CHAPTER 3

REAL MADRID IN THE ATTACKING PHASE

REAL MADRID'S FORMATIONS DURING THE ATTACKING PHASE

Real Madrid used the 4-2-3-1 formation during the attacking phase in almost every match they played. However, several variations of this formation took place during the build up play. Some variations of the 4-2-3-1 formation were used only temporarily lasting for just 1 or 2 attacks, while some others lasted for longer periods during the matches.

They had to take advantage of the strong points in each of the formations to cause problems for the opposition and prevent being predictable. The variations mainly came from the wingers' flexibility who took up various positions on the field. The rest of the players had to adapt to the wingers' positioning in order to retain the team's balance and to create the correct shapes.

In some cases, the change in formation came from the holding midfielder dropping into a deeper position, (a central defender's role) but this also was not a permanent situation.

Basic formation: The width is created by the full backs

Diagram 17.0 presents the basic formation for the team. The wingers took up positions towards the centre and the width was provided by the full back's advanced positions. This formation helped Real Madrid to outnumber the opposition in the centre of the field.

If the opposing team forced their wide players towards the centre to try and counter the numerical advantage, the ball was directed to the full backs who would have plenty of available space to exploit.

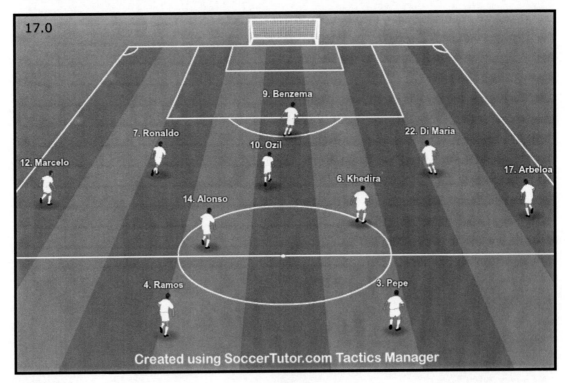

THE WIDTH ON THE LEFT IS CREATED BY THE WINGER

On diagram 17.1, Ronaldo takes up a position near the sideline and creates width on the left and Arbeloa provides the width on the right. Marcelo moves towards the centre to provide balance. This positioning of Marcelo enables Alonso to move into the centre and in some cases he would take up a more advanced position.

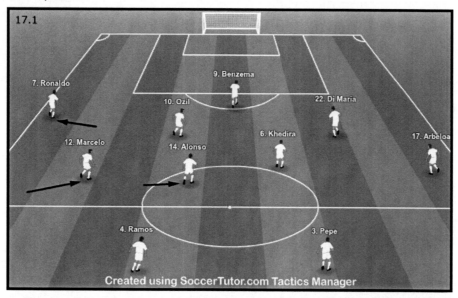

On diagram 17.2, we have a similar situation to the previous one. Ronaldo is again near the sideline. Due to Benzema's positioning towards the left, Ozil is placed in the centre and Di Maria moves forward and towards the left.

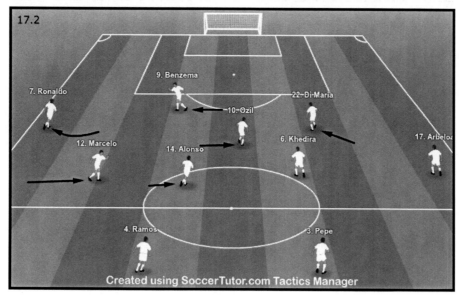

THE WIDTH ON THE RIGHT IS CREATED BY THE WINGER

On diagram 17.3, Di Maria is the one who places himself near the sideline on the right. Arbeloa moves towards the centre into a position which provides balance. Khedira moves higher up the pitch and Alonso moves into the centre.

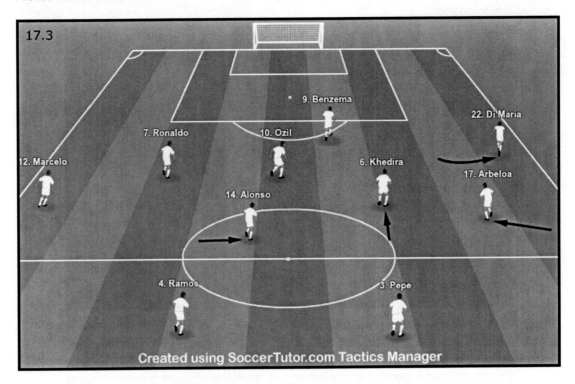

PLAYING WITH 2 FORWARDS

In situations where Mourinho used both Benzema and Higuain in the starting 11, Benzema was placed towards the right, but during most phases of play Real Madrid would have 2 forwards. Ronaldo moved towards the centre and Ozil towards the right side in a more attack minded formation.

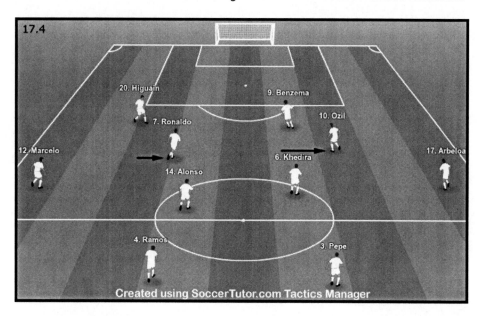

When the team used the formation shown in diagram 17.5, there were times when Ozil moved near to the sideline and provided width. This forced Khedira higher up the pitch and Arbeloa towards the centre.

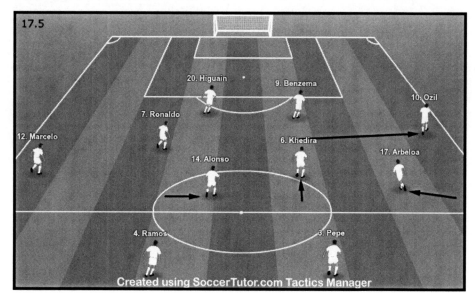

BOTH THE WINGER AND THE FULL BACK CREATE WIDTH

On diagrams 17.6 and 17.7, either Ronaldo and Marcelo or Di Maria and Arbeloa are placed near the sideline. Ozil shifts towards the left and towards the right respectively.

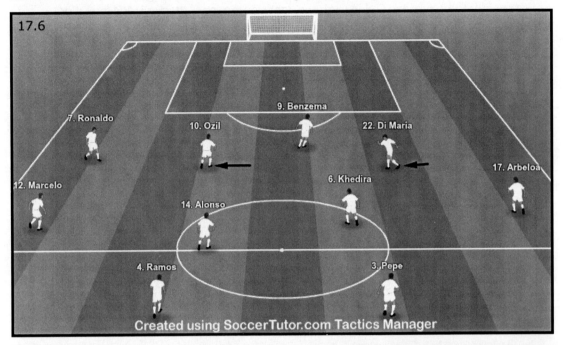

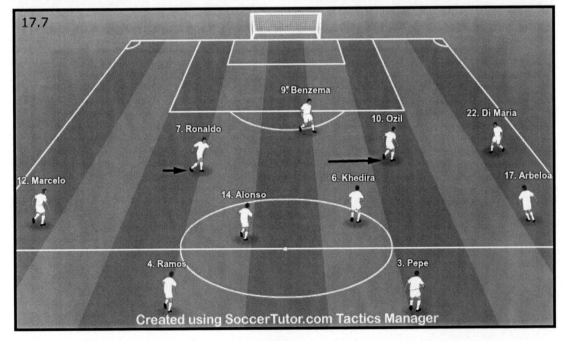

THE CENTRE FORWARD DROPS DEEP ON THE STRONG SIDE

On diagrams 17.8 and 17.9, both the winger and the full back are placed near the sideline. The attacking midfielder is away from the strong side. This results in the centre forward (Benzema) dropping deep in order to provide an extra passing option for the ball carrier.

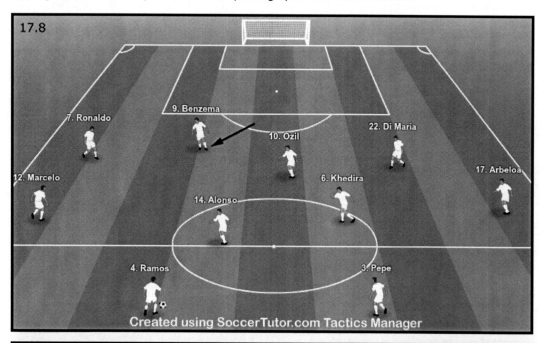

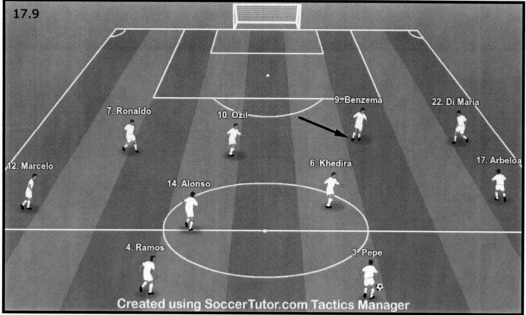

CENTRAL DEFENDER BUILD UP PLAY FROM THE BACK

Ramos in a central position

On diagrams 17.10, 17.11 and 17.12, the formation of Real Madrid changes as Alonso drops into a central defender's position to receive the ball free of marking (diagram 17.10) or to retain the team's balance.

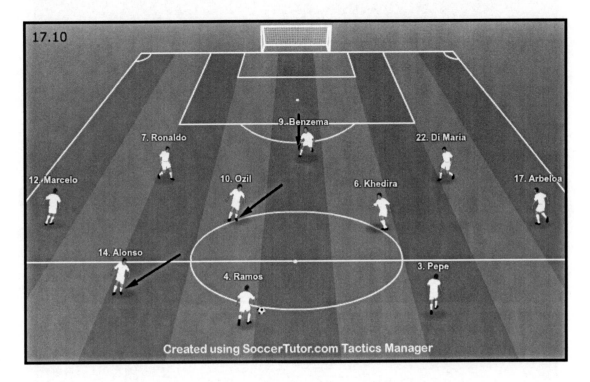

Ramos' forward run with the ball on the left

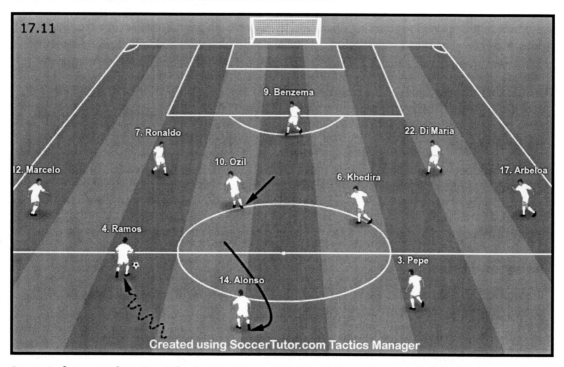

Pepe's forward run with the ball on the right

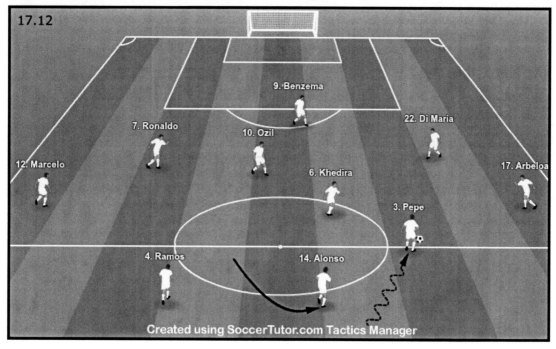

THE 3 STAGES OF THE BUILD UP & THE TARGET AREAS

Real Madrid's aim during the attacking phase was to create as many situations as possible which led to an attempt on goal. That is why they used a mix of different types of build up play; short passing combinations, long passes towards the weak side and in behind the opposition's defensive line.

The attacking phase includes all the team's actions when they have possession of the ball, with the aim of scoring a goal. This can be separated into 3 stages:

The first stage:

This stage includes all the actions taken to move the ball forward from the defenders to the midfielders or in some cases directly to the forwards dropping into a midfielder's position.

Real Madrid used mainly vertical and diagonal passes during this stage. In several cases they skipped the first stage and tried to move directly to the second or even the third stage by using long passes.

The second phase:

This stage includes all the actions taken to move the ball into areas where the final pass towards the attacking players was easy to make.

Real Madrid sought to create superiority in numbers, creating and exploiting free spaces down the flanks inn order to play the ball into the 'A' and 'B' areas (Diagram 17.13). They also used long passes towards the flanks when the opposition closed down the space in the central zone.

To get the ball into the 'C' area, Real used passing combinations in the central zone or driving runs towards the centre by the wingers and sometimes by the full backs.

The third phase:

This stage includes the final pass (diagonal or vertical) or cross into the box for the attacking players to take a shot or header on goal.

Real Madrid used low crosses and high out swinging crosses from the 'A' area, which would target Benzema/ Higuain, Ronaldo or even Khedira in the penalty area.

From the 'B' area, the team used in swinging crosses and from the 'C' area, the players would try to make killer passes towards the attacking players or attempt a direct shot on goal.

THE TARGET AREAS

Diagram 17.13 presents the 3 target areas for Real Madrid's build up play.

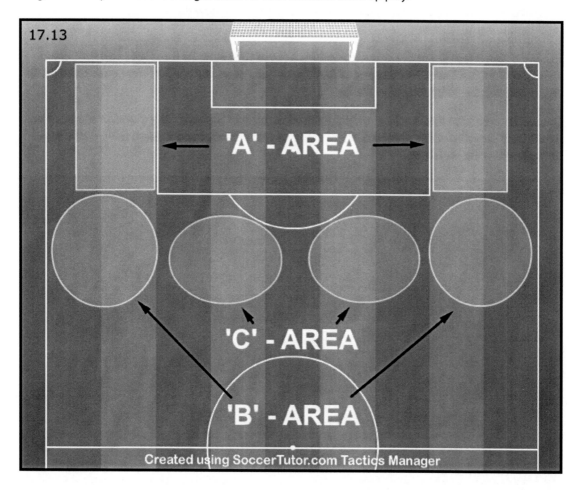

RETAINING THE TEAM'S BALANCE DURING THE BUILD UP

In order for Real Madrid to retain its balance during the attacking phase, the players worked very well in collaboration. The diagrams to follow show some examples of how the Madrid players worked together during this phase.

Either the centre forward or the attacking midfielder used to exploit the free space created behind the opposition's full backs. This was one of Real's main aims when the wingers were positioned in the centre and dropped back to receive the ball.

The centre forward or the attacking midfielder used to move to the top of the rhombus shape when the wingers provided width and the ball was in the central defender's possession towards the side. Both situations are presented.

Diagrams 18.0 and 18.1 present the usual positions of the centre forward and the attacking midfielder. This positioning enabled Real to always have an available player near the strong side.

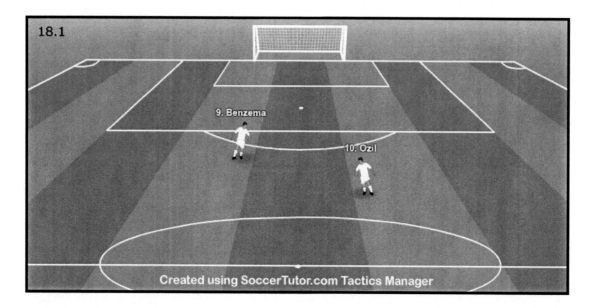

On diagram 18.2, Ozil moves closer to the strong side than the centre forward, attacking the free space Ronaldo creates on the left.

POSITIONING: CREATING THE CORRECT SHAPES

On diagram 18.3, it is Benzema who exploits the free space that Ronaldo creates.

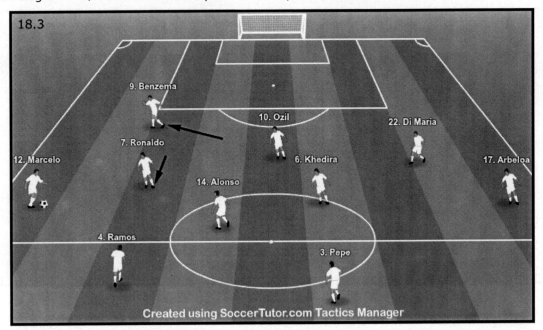

On diagram 18.4, Ozil moves into a supporting position at the top of the rhombus shape as Ronaldo stays near the sideline.

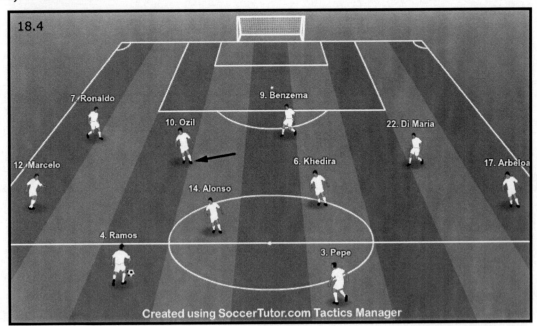

On diagram 18.5, as Benzema is closer to the strong side than Ozil, he moves to provide a passing option at the top of the rhombus shape. This move affects Di Maria as he moves to take up the centre forward's position vacated by Benzema.

On diagram 18.6, as Benzema drops back, Ronaldo moves to take up the centre forward's position.

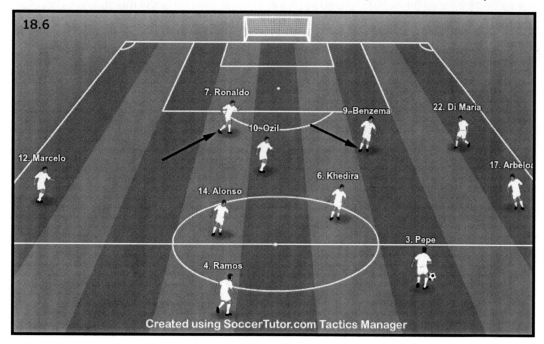

MOVEMENT WITH AND WITHOUT THE BALL

As Ramos moved forward with the ball towards the left, Alonso dropped deeper to retain the team's balance. This move affected Ozil's positioning as he also drops deeper to take up Alonso's position and move to the top of the rhombus shape.

On diagram 18.7.1, Ozil drops deep and takes up a position at the side of the rhombus with Ronaldo at the top.

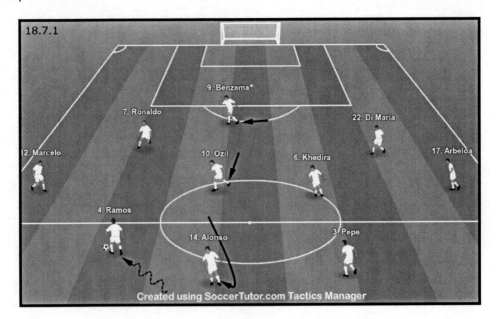

On diagram 18.8, Ozil moves to the top of the rhombus as Ronaldo is placed near to the sideline. Khedira provides support from the inside.

When Ronaldo played as a centre forward, Benzema or Higuain moved towards the left.

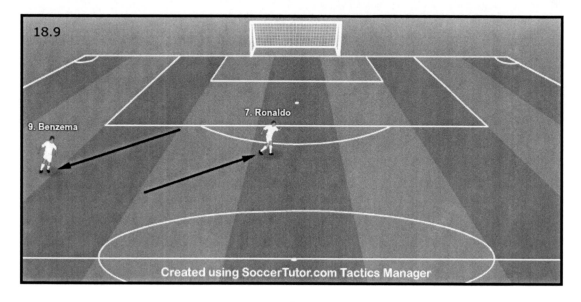

FORWARDS: ROTATING POSITIONS

Benzema moves to the top of the rhombus shape.

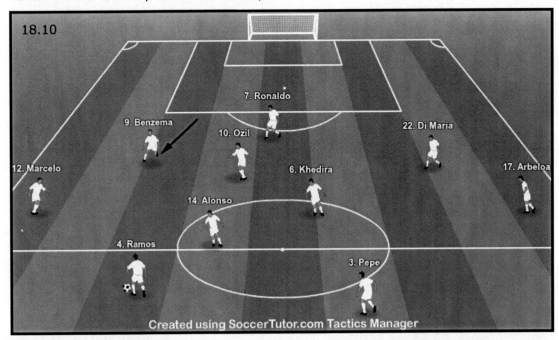

On diagram 18.11, Benzema moves towards the sideline as Ronaldo has a central position.

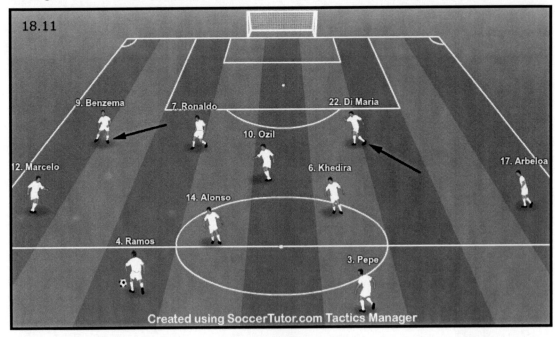

CHAPTER 4

REAL MADRID DURING THE BUILD UP

REAL MADRID DURING THE BUILD UP PLAY ON THE LEFT SIDE WITH THE WIDTH CREATED BY THE FULL BACK

In order for the build up play from the back to be effective, Real Madrid's players looked to create the correct shapes. These shapes were the rhombus and the triangle and through them the players used a variety of passing combinations. The rhombus and the triangle can be seen easily in Madrid's various formations during the build up play.

The diagrams to follow show some of the shapes which were created during the attacking phase (especially during the build up from the back) in all the various formations used. There are also diagrams which show the passing combinations which were most frequently used through each particular shape.

On diagram 18.12, the build up starts with Ramos in possession. Marcelo creates width at left back and the correct shape is created by Ronaldo taking up a position at the top of the rhombus and by Alonso providing support towards the inside.

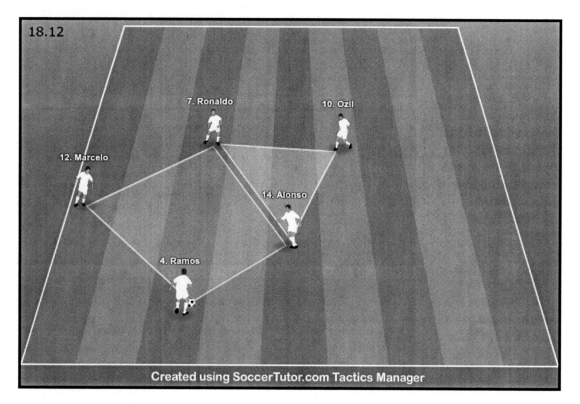

On diagram 18.13, there is a combination between Marcelo and Ronaldo which leads to Marcelo receiving towards the centre.

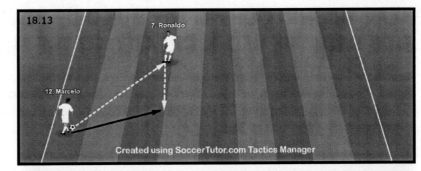

On diagram 18.14, Marcelo moves towards the centre again and receives the pass from Ronaldo.

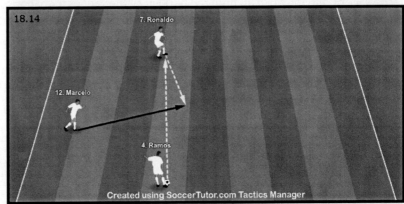

On diagram 18.15, Ronaldo drops back to create space as well as superiority in numbers around the ball zone and after receiving he passes the ball to Alonso.

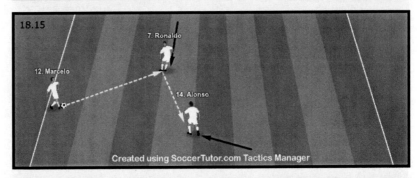

Ronaldo drops back again. Ozil makes a move in behind him to exploit the free space and receives the pass from Marcelo.

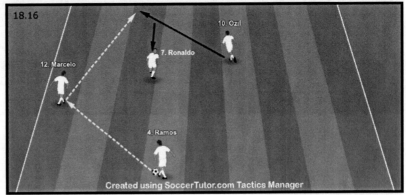

On diagram 18.17, Ronaldo and Marcelo make opposite movements. As Ronaldo creates space behind his back, Marcelo takes advantage of it by moving forward and receiving the pass from Ramos.

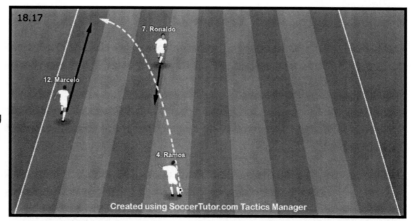

On diagram 18.18, Alonso is the man in possession in a situation which usually took place near the opposition's penalty area. Ozil plays a first time pass to Ronaldo who has already moved towards the opposition's goal.

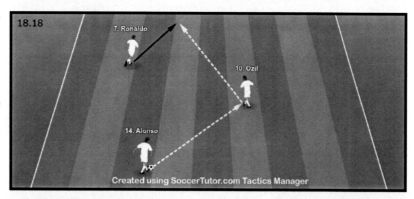

On diagram 18.19, Ronaldo receives and moves towards the centre. Ozil makes the movement towards the left side to exploit the free space.

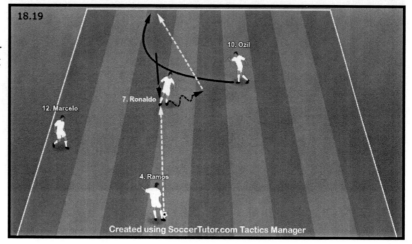

NUMERICAL SUPERIORITY IN THE CENTRE

Real Madrid used different passing combinations depending on the formation they were using during the game. The formation used could last for several attacks, but also change at any point.

In the diagrams below, the team's wingers are placed towards the centre in order to create superiority in numbers in midfield. This forced the opposition's full backs to move towards the centre to mark Ronaldo and Di Maria. This positioning created free space down the flanks for the Real Madrid full backs to exploit.

The wingers would drop deep several times during the match to outnumber the opposition near the ball zone and help the team's passing game. When the wingers dropped deep it created space on the flanks to be exploited by the centre forward or the attacking midfielder.

On diagram 18.20, Ramos is the man in possession towards the left. Marcelo, Ronaldo and Alonso create a rhombus shape and provide Ramos with 3 passing options.

DEFENSIVE MIDFIELDER'S PASSING OPTIONS

On diagram 18.21, Marcelo receives the pass near the sideline. Ronaldo drops back to outnumber the opposition near the ball zone while at the same time creating space for Ozil who moves in behind the opposition full back (No.2).

Ronaldo is able to receive unmarked and pass the ball back to Alonso. Alonso has 3 passing options in order to switch the play.

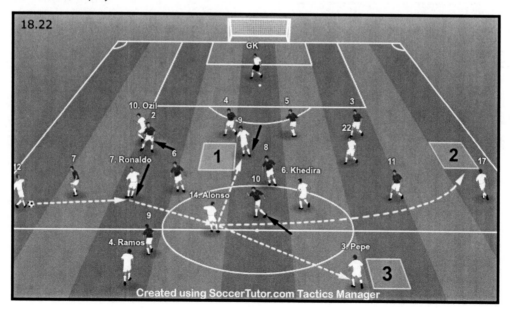

FULL BACK'S MOVEMENT INSIDE

On diagram 18.23, Ronaldo moves to provide support for the man in possession. Ozil makes a move to exploit the free space created behind No.2.

Marcelo passes to Ronaldo and makes a move to receive the pass back.

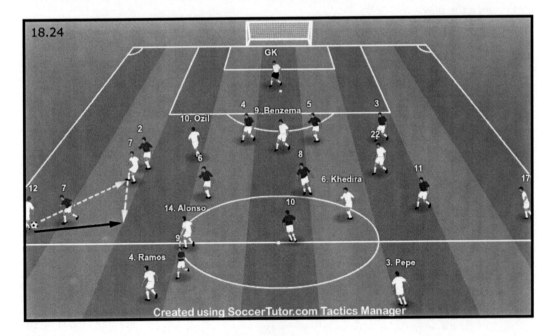

After receiving, Marcelo dribbles the ball towards the centre and has space to play in before he is closed down. Marcelo has 2 options; to pass to Ronaldo (option 1) who moves down the flank or to Benzema (option 2) who provides a passing option inside. Benzema would have the chance to pass directly to Ozil who has made a run in behind the opposition's defence.

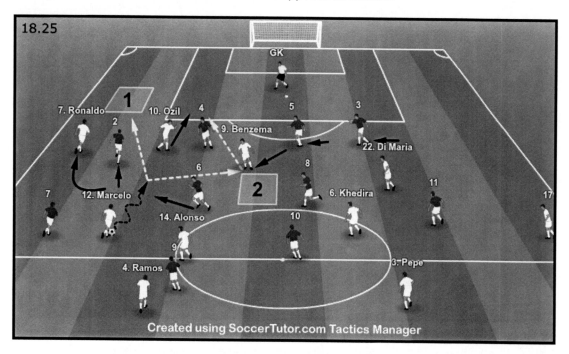

 ASSESSMENT:

When Marcelo received the ball near the sideline, Ronaldo rarely made a movement to receive down the line. Instead he stayed in a position towards the centre and left the space down the flank to be exploited by the full back, the centre forward or the attacking midfielder.

When Marcelo was in a more central position, then Ronaldo would make more runs down the flank.

CREATING SPACE TO RECEIVE ON THE LEFT FLANK

On diagram 18.26, Ronaldo's movement deep into midfield drags the opposition right back (No.2) out of position. Ozil moves towards the sideline to receive in the available free space.

Ozil receives the pass as Benzema and Di Maria move to receive the cross in the box.

On diagram 18.28, in a similar situation to the previous one, No.4 tracks Ozil's run.

When Ozil receives, he is under pressure from No.4 and he is not able to turn towards the opposition's goal.

In this situation, Marcelo moves forward to receive down the flank (option 1), Ronaldo moves forward towards the opposition's goal (option 2) and Alonso supports Ozil from behind (option 3) to provide safety.

CENTRE FORWARD: MOVEMENT INTO 'CHANNELS'

On diagram 18.31, Ozil is away from the ball zone, so Benzema tries to exploit the free space created by Ronaldo's movement.

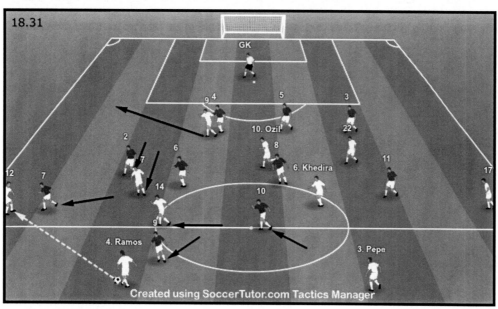

Benzema receives Marcelo's pass down the flank and as he is very effective in one on ones near the sideline. Ozil and Di Maria move into the box to receive a potential cross and Ronaldo moves into a position just outside the box. Benzema can cross the ball (option 1), pass to Ronaldo (option 2) or dribble towards the centre and shoot on goal (option 3).

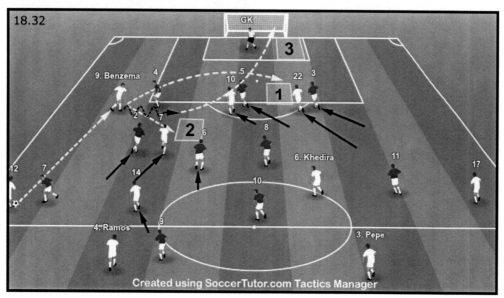

 ## ASSESSMENT:

When Ozil was far enough away from the ball zone, the centre forward (Benzema or Higuain) would move into the channel to take advantage of the free space behind the opposition's right back.

This was seen mostly on the left side because Ronaldo would often take up a central position.

RECEIVING WITH YOUR BACK TO GOAL

On diagram 18.33, Ronaldo drops back and receives the vertical pass from Ramos. The right back (No.2) does not follow his movement this time and leaves No.6 to take over the marking.

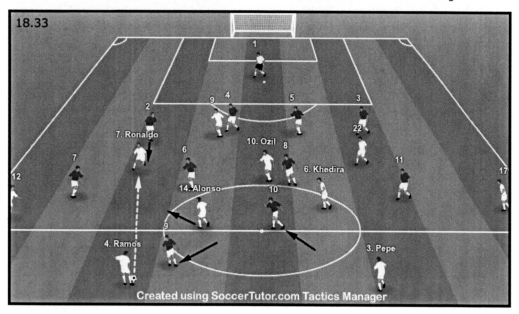

As Ronaldo finds space and turns towards the opposition's goal, Real reach the third stage of the build up and Benzema (option 1) together with Di Maria (option 2) make their runs to receive the final pass in behind the defensive line. Ronaldo can also make a longer pass towards Arbeloa (option 3) in case the passes towards Di Maria and Benzema are blocked.

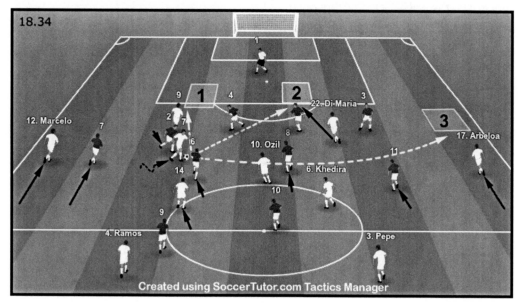

Here the situation is different as the opponents squeezed the space in the midfield and Ronaldo was double or triple marked when receiving. When this happened he used to receive and pass the ball back allowing the team to exploit the free space available on the flanks.

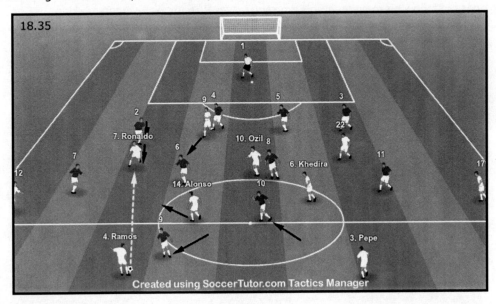

On diagram 18.35 however, when No.2 follows Ronaldo's deep movement. Benzema realises the tactical context and moves to provide a passing option in front of Ronaldo.

Ronaldo passes first time to Benzema and spins away from his marker to make a run towards the sideline to receive Benzema's pass (option 1). If the pass to Ronaldo is not possible, Benzema has the security to pass the ball back to Ozil (option 2).

 # ASSESSMENT:

When a pass was directed to Ronaldo and he had available space towards the inside of the field, he used to turn towards the centre and drive with the ball diagonally looking for the final pass or a shot on goal.

In these tactical situations, Ozil often used to move towards the left to create space for Ronaldo and also exploit the free space Ronaldo created for him.

On diagram 18.37, as the pass is directed to Ronaldo, both No.7 and No.6 move to double mark him. Alonso moves across to provide a passing option.

Alonso receives the pass back from Ronaldo and has 3 available options to pass the ball forwards.

LONG PASSES TO ADVANCING FULL BACKS

On diagram 18.39, Marcelo and Ronaldo move in opposite directions. With these movements space is created down the flank as No.2 follows Ronaldo and the pass is directed to Marcelo.

Marcelo crosses the ball into the box targeting Benzema, Ozil or Di Maria.

 # ASSESSMENT:

There were times when the defensive midfielder (Alonso) took the place of Ramos at the base of the rhombus shape on the left.

The combinations used during the attacking phase were still the same when this happened.

RHOMBUS/DIAMOND SHAPE IN THE CENTRAL ZONE

In the diagrams below (18.41 and 18.42), the correct shapes are created by the defensive midfielder Alonso taking the place of the central defender at the base of the rhombus. Marcelo is on the left, Khedira on the right and Ronaldo on top. The passing combinations shown did not change significantly.

The rhombus shape is created by the shift of Khedira towards the left.

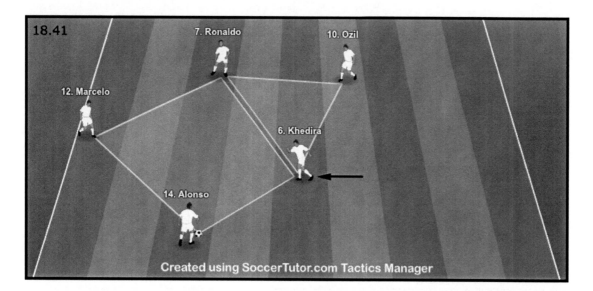

On diagram 18.42, the rhombus shape is created by Ozil dropping deep into a defensive midfielder's position.

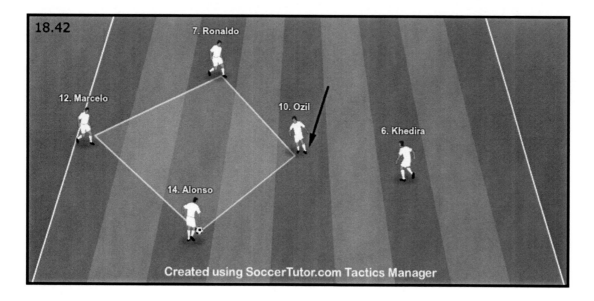

DEFENSIVE MIDFIELDER'S POSITIONING

On diagram 18.43, Ramos is placed in the centre of the field. As the 2 opposition forwards block off the passing lanes towards Ozil and Khedira, Alonso drops deep to receive free of marking.

As soon as the ball reaches Alonso, Marcelo, Ronaldo and Ozil provide passing options using the rhombus shape on the left side of the pitch.

On diagram 18.45, the correct shape is created by the movements of Ronaldo and Khedira

STARTING THE BUILD UP THROUGH THE CENTRE WITH THE WIDTH CREATED BY THE FULL BACKS

With Ramos as the man in possession, the correct shape in the centre of the field was created by the 2 defensive midfielders and Ozil on top of the rhombus. The passing combinations used were simple because they were in a critical part of the field where the potential loss of possession could cause a lot of problems.

On diagram 19.0, the rhombus shape is created in the centre of the field.

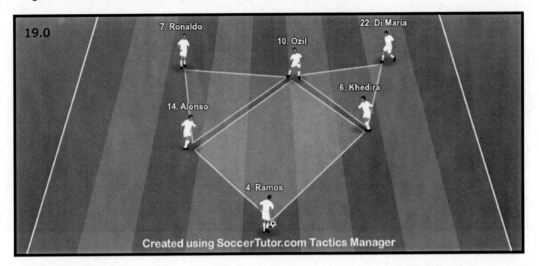

Ozil usually looked for utilise the space between the opposition's defence and midfield line. He sought to receive the ball behind the midfielders. However, if the passing lanes were blocked, Ozil dropped back to create superiority in numbers around the ball zone. In this situation presented,

Ozil would drop back to receive and pass back to either Khedira or Alonso.

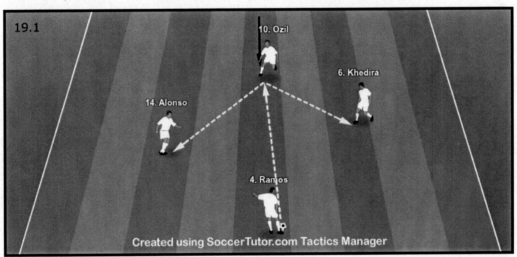

RETAINING POSSESSION IN THE CENTRAL ZONE

On diagram 19.2, No.9 and No.10 block off the direct passes towards Khedira and Alonso. Ozil then drops deep to provide a passing option for the man in possession. The ball is passed to Khedira through Ozil. Khedira has 2 available passing options to develop the build up play.

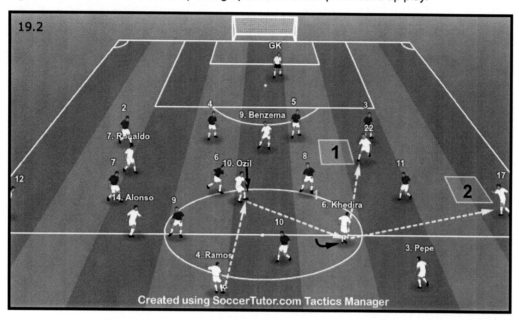

On diagram 19.3, the ball is this time directed to Alonso through Ozil who drops deep again. Alonso can pass the ball to Ronaldo (option 1) or Marcelo (option 2).

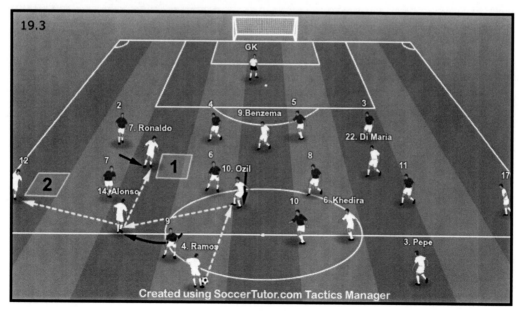

ALONSO'S ROLE: COVERING IN DEFENCE

On diagram 19.4, Ramos decides to dribble the ball towards the left side. Alonso drops into a position which provides support and helps retain the team's balance. Ozil drops deep to create the correct shape and Benzema moves to take up Ozil's position

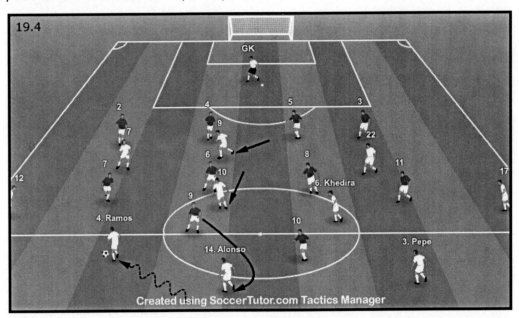

On diagram 19.5, Ramos makes the same move. As both Ronaldo and Marcelo are placed near the sideline, Ozil moves to the top of the rhombus. Khedira also moves towards the strong side.

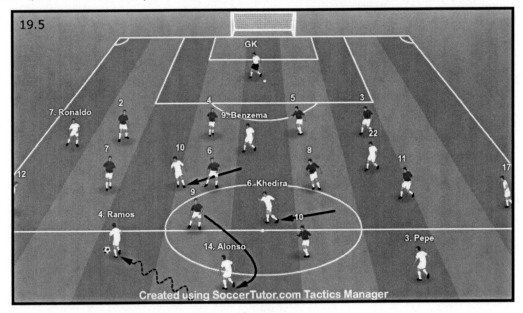

DEVELOPING THE BUILD UP PLAY THROUGH THE CENTRE

When the defensive midfielder (Alonso) was the man in possession in the centre of the field, the rhombus was created by Ronaldo, Ozil and the centre forward, who was placed at the top of the shape.

On diagram 19.6, Alonso has possession of the ball in the centre of the field.

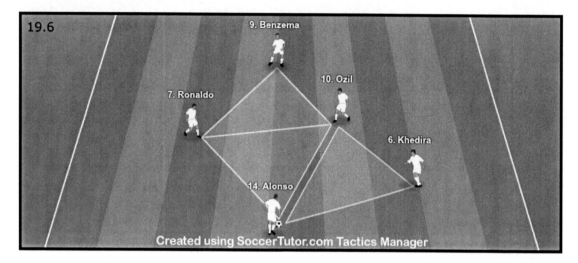

On diagram 19.7, there is a combination in the centre of the field. Alonso makes a vertical pass. Benzema plays it back to Ozil. The new man in possession dribbles the ball towards the centre, while Benzema and Ronaldo move diagonally to create and exploit the free space.

Ozil receives and passes to Ronaldo. He then makes a diagonal run into the free space. Benzema also makes a move to receive.

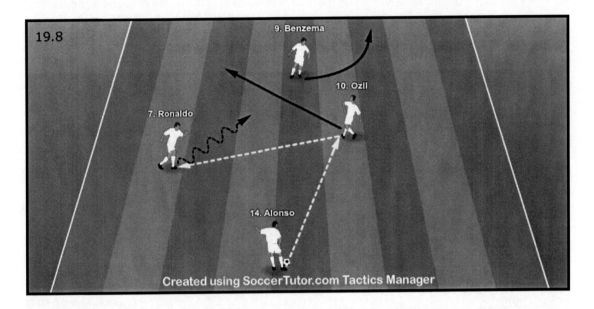

Benzema passes the ball to Di Maria this time and moves diagonally. Ronaldo also makes a diagonal movement. All 3 situations can lead to the final pass.

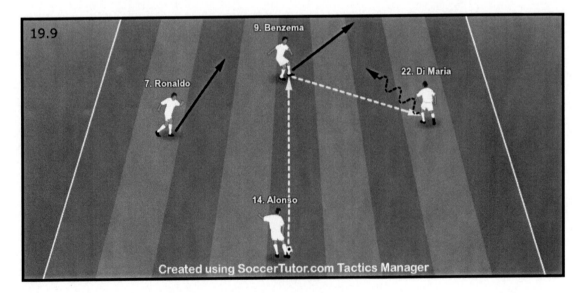

DEFENSIVE MIDFIELDER AT THE BASE OF THE RHOMBUS SHAPE

On diagram 19.10, the positioning of the opposition's forwards blocks off the potential passes towards Ozil and Khedira. Alonso drops deep to provide a passing option and receives the ball. The situation can develop as the ones presented before as Ramos takes up Alonso's position at the base of the rhombus.

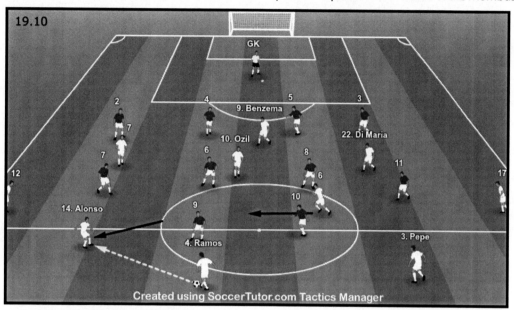

Alonso receives the pass from Ramos.

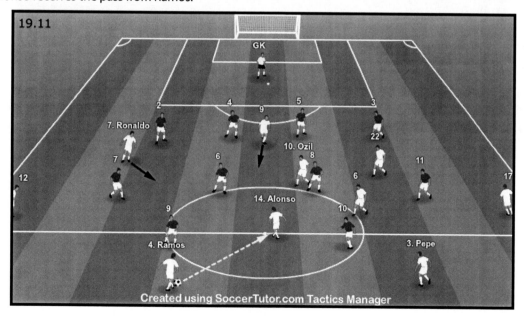

The pass is directed to Ronaldo who drives the ball inside. Benzema moves in behind No.2's back (option 1) and Di Maria makes a diagonal run between No.3 and No.5 (option 2). Both provide passing options for the ball carrier. Ronaldo can also try a shot on goal.

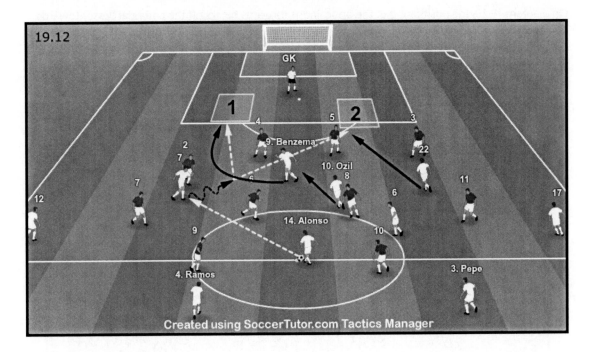

 ## ASSESSMENT:

Alonso was the link player between the defenders and the forwards. So when he received a pass in a central position, the wingers as well as the centre forward and attacking midfielder would move into a passing lane to receive the ball.

DECISION MAKING IN THE FINAL THIRD

Alonso passes the ball to Benzema who passes first time to Ronaldo.

The situation develops like the previous one. This time the diagram also presents the movements made by the Real players in order for the team to get ready for the negative transition. Alonso is the man who provides safety, while the central defenders move forward and the full-backs converge towards the centre.

EXAMPLE 2

On diagram 19.15, Ozil receives the pass back from Benzema.

Real's attacking midfielder dribbles the ball towards the centre and has 2 available passing options, to Ronaldo (option 1) and Benzema (option 2). He can also try a shot on goal (option 3).

EXAMPLE 3

On diagram 19.17, the ball reaches Di Maria.

The new man in possession begins a driving run towards the centre. Benzema (option 2) moves behind No.3 who contests Di Maria. Ronaldo (option 1) makes a diagonal run to receive in the free space while Ozil (option 3) provides a passing option outside the box. Di Maria can also shoot at goal (option 4).

EXAMPLE 4

On diagram 19.19, Ozil receives the ball from Benzema.

As the 4 defenders have taken up positions towards the centre, Ronaldo (option 1) and Benzema (option 2) use diagonal runs while Di Maria (option 3) opens up towards the right. Ozil can either pass to one of them or shoot on goal (option 4).

EXAMPLE 5

Finally, on diagram 19.21 there is a combination between Ozil and Ronaldo which was used numerous times throughout the season. Ozil moves towards the passing lane, receives and plays a first time ball to Ronaldo who moves diagonally towards the free space Benzema has created. The same combination was used between Benzema and Ozil when Ozil was placed towards the left side.

 ## ASSESSMENT:

When Benzema dropped back to receive this would create space behind him and Ronaldo would almost always move to take advantage of it.

STARTING THE BUILD UP ON THE RIGHT WITH THE WIDTH CREATED BY THE FULL BACK

When the build up play took place on the right and the width was created by the full back, the rhombus shape was created by Khedira, Arbeloa and Di Maria at the top. Pepe was the man in possession at the base of the shape.

On diagram 19.22, the build up play takes place on the right with Pepe as the man in possession.

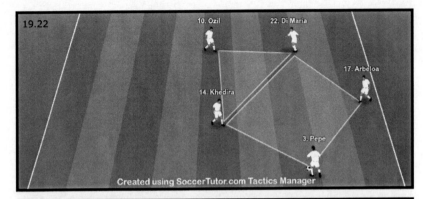

As Di Maria drops deep to receive, he creates space behind. Ozil moves to exploit this available space and receives the long pass from Pepe.

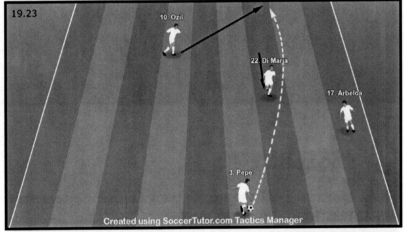

On diagram 19.24, Di Maria drops back, receives and passes to Arbeloa. After the pass he makes a move towards the sideline to create and exploit the space. Ozil moves to provide a passing option.

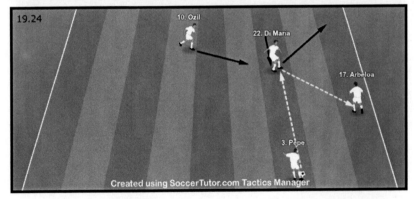

On diagram 19.25, when Arbeloa receives the pass, Di Maria moves towards the side to receive. Kaka moves into the space created and receives the ball.

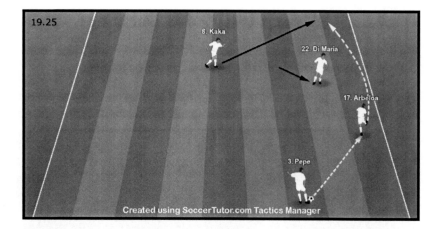

This time, Di Maria drops deep to outnumber the opposition around the ball zone and receive. This action also creates space behind his back.

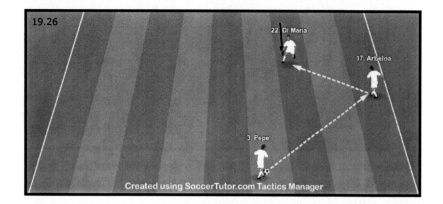

Di Maria and Arbeloa make opposite movements here. Space is created by Di Maria as he drags the opposition full back out of position, so Pepe passes the ball to Arbeloa.

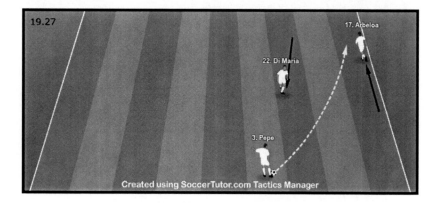

THE RIGHT WINGER DROPPING DEEP TO MAINTAIN POSSESSION

The diagrams to follow present situations that frequently took place on the right side during matches. Di Maria is placed centrally and the width is created by Arbeloa.

On diagram 19.28, the pass from Pepe is played to Arbeloa. Di Maria drops back to receive as well as to create space for Benzema. The opposing team shifts towards the right side to retain cohesion.

No.3 does not follow Di Maria's movement, so he is able to receive the ball free of marking. However, due to this, little space is created behind Di Maria's back for Benzema to exploit. The new ball carrier (Di Maria) has 3 available passing options.

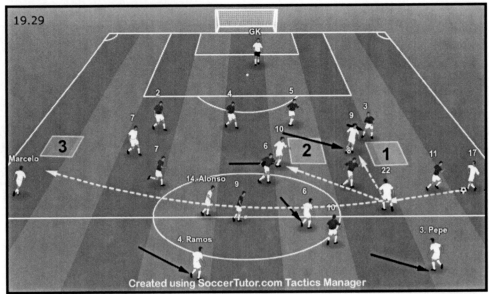

CENTRE FORWARD RECEIVING ON THE FLANK

On diagram 19.30, No.3 does follow Di Maria's movement this time. Space is created for Benzema to exploit and he makes a move behind No.3's back in order to receive.

The pass is directed to Benzema who dribbles the ball towards the sideline. Benzema had great ability in one against ones near the sideline, so Ronaldo and Ozil move into the box to take up positions for a potential cross.

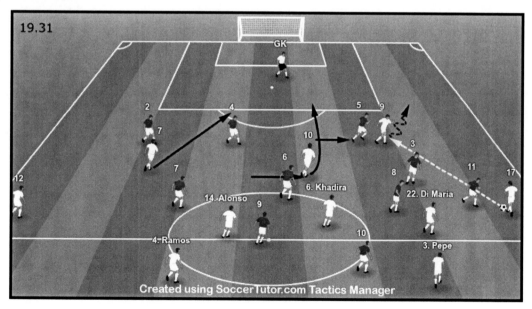

On diagram 19.32, Benzema is ready to get past No.5 and cross the ball into the box. Ronaldo and Ozil time their runs into the box. Di Maria moves into a position outside the box and the rest of the Madrid players move up to take positions which retain the team's compactness.

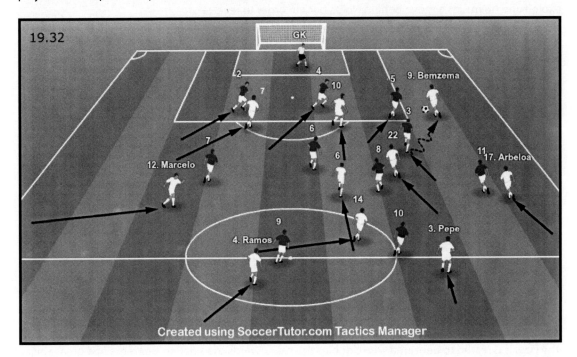

MOVEMENT WITHOUT THE BALL: CREATING SPACE

On diagram 19.33, Di Maria makes a move towards the sideline. Benzema moves into a supporting position in front of Arbeloa taking advantage of the space Di Maria has created.

Di Maria receives the pass from Arbeloa and Benzema makes a move towards the sideline exploiting the free space to receive, as well as to create space for Di Maria to move into.

Di Maria makes a driving run towards the inside. Ronaldo (option 1) moves diagonally in order to receive the final pass. Di Maria can also switch the play with a long ball to Marcelo (option 2).

DIAGONAL RUNS IN THE FINAL THIRD

On diagram 19.36, Di Maria again moves towards the sideline. The advanced position of Khedira enables him to take advantage of the space created behind the opposition's left back and becomes an extra man for Real in attack. Benzema again moves to provide a passing option inside with his back to goal.

As the opposition central defender (No.5) moves to mark Khedira, Benzema is left free of marking. He receives the pass from Arbeloa and has the chance to turn towards the opposition's goal.

Benzema dribbles the ball towards the inside and can play a final pass to either Ronaldo (option 1) or to Khedira (option 2).

 ## ASSESSMENT:

When the build up play took place near the sidelines and the attacking midfielder was far enough from the ball zone, the centre forward (Benzema or Higuain) used to either drop back or move towards this sideline to help the team develop their attacking moves.

CENTRAL MIDFIELDER'S FORWARD RUNS

On diagram 19.39, the same situation takes place.

This time the central defender (No.5) follows Benzema. The pass from Arbeloa is directed down the line to Khedira who attacks the free space behind No.3.

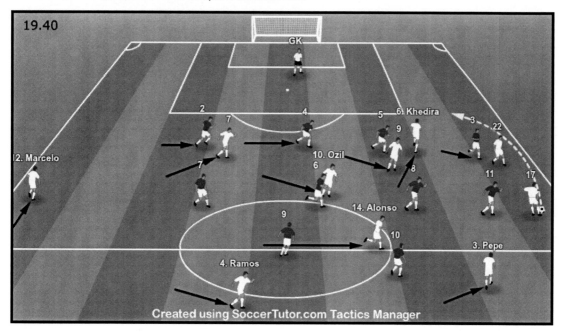

On diagram 19.41, Real Madrid's players move to take up positions inside and outside of the box. Alonso, together with the full backs and Di Maria prepare for the team's negative transition.

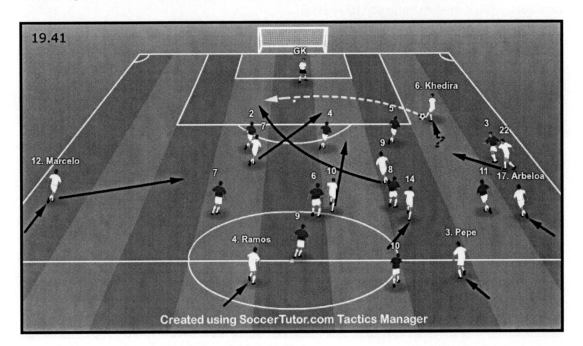

DEEP MOVEMENT: CREATING SPACE IN BEHIND

On diagram 19.42, Di Maria drops back to receive and creates space for Ozil.

Pepe makes a long pass towards the free space on the right. Ozil receives and moves forward. Ronaldo and Benzema move into the box to receive the potential cross, while Di Maria takes up a position outside the box. The rest of the Real Madrid players retain the team's balance and are prepared for the transition.

EXAMPLE 2: USING A LONG PASS

On diagram 19.44, the same situation takes place in a different way as Pepe's long ball targets Benzema and Ozil can exploit Di Maria's movement to make a run in behind No.3.

The ball reaches Ozil free in space after Benzema's header. Ronaldo and Benzema move into the box to meet a potential cross.

On diagram 19.46, Di Maria drops deep, receives and moves towards the inside in the available space. Ronaldo (option 1) and Benzema (option 2) move diagonally to receive the final pass.

CENTRAL MIDFIELD PASSING OPTIONS

On diagram 19.47, Di Maria drops deep and receives, but this time there is no available space towards the inside.

Di Maria plays the ball back to Khedira as he is being triple marked by the opposition. The new man in possession can pass to Benzema (option 1) or switch the play by making a long pass to Marcelo (option 2).

2 v 1 ATTACKING DOWN THE FLANK

On diagram 19.49, Di Maria receives and passes to Arbeloa who moves forward.

On diagram 19.50, as No.3 moves to contest Arbeloa, Di Maria makes a run down the line and receives the ball in behind the left back.

Di Maria turns inside and puts an in swinging cross into the penalty area. The targets are Benzema and Ronaldo who time their runs to meet the cross and shoot / head at goal.

CENTRAL MIDFIELD PASSING OPTIONS (2)

On diagram 19.52, Arbeloa makes a forward run and creates space for Di Maria who drops back and receives free of marking. Ozil moves to provide support in front of him and Khedira behind him.

As Ozil is being marked, the pass is directed to Khedira who has 3 passing options.

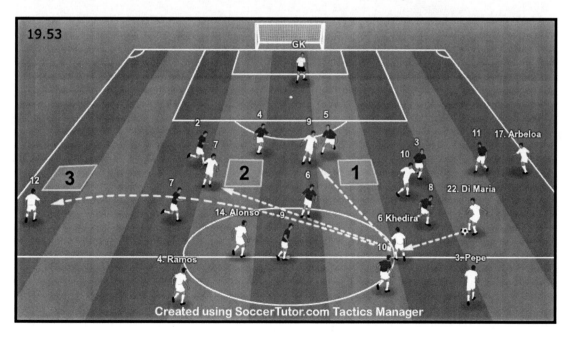

CORRECT POSITIONING WHEN THE CENTRAL MIDFIELDER HAS POSSESSION

Diagram 19.54 presents how the correct shape was created when Khedira was the man in possession and at the base of the rhombus. In this case, the movements and the passing combinations between Real Madrid players did not differ significantly.

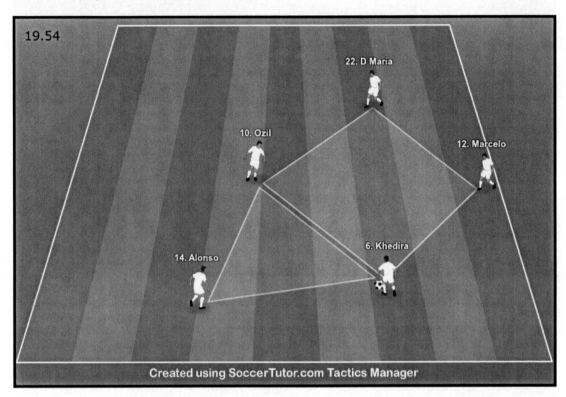

STARTING THE BUILD UP ON THE LEFT WITH BOTH THE FULL BACK AND THE WINGER CREATING WIDTH

When the build up started on the left and the width was created by both the full back and the winger, there was a shift of the attacking midfielder towards the same side in order to take up a position at the top of the rhombus shape.

On diagram 20.0, both Ronaldo and Marcelo are positioned near the sideline. This forces Ozil to move into the position at the top of the rhombus shape.

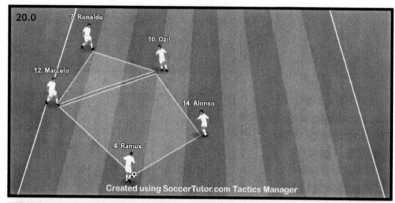

Marcelo, after receiving the ball, plays a one-two combination with Ronaldo.

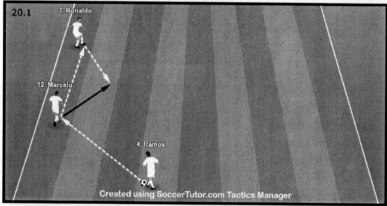

On diagram 20.2, there is another combination between Marcelo and Ronaldo. Marcelo passes to Ronaldo and as Ronaldo dribbles inside, Marcelo makes an overlapping run.

On diagram 20.3, Ronaldo receives and dribbles towards the centre. Ozil makes a run behind the back of Ronaldo to take advantage of the space he has created and provides a passing option.

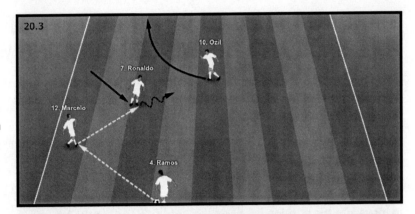

Ramos passes to Ozil, who has dropped deep to help outnumber the opposition near the ball zone and receive. Ozil then passes back to Alonso.

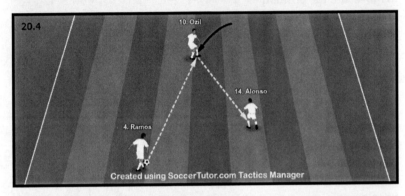

Diagram 20.5 shows a combination between 3 players. Ozil receives, passes to Ronaldo and then continues his run towards the sideline (creating and exploiting the free space). The new man in possession makes a driving run towards the centre looking to shoot or make a final pass.

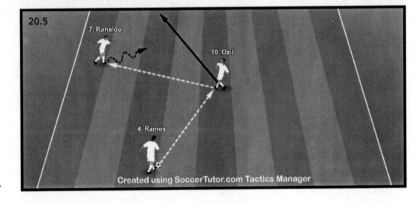

 # ASSESSMENT:

When both Ronaldo and Marcelo were placed near the sideline they would attempt to stretch the opposition with the rhombus shape being created by Ozil's movement across towards the left side.

2 v 2 ATTACKING DOWN THE LEFT FLANK

On diagram 20.6, the pass is directed to Marcelo. There is a shift of the opposing team towards the left side.

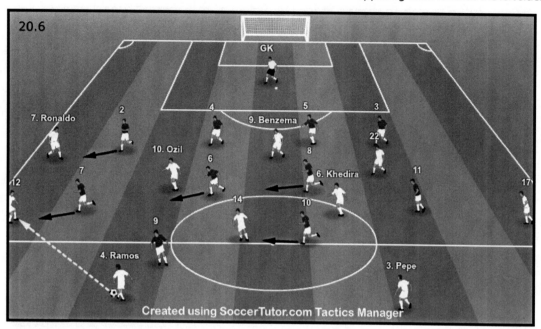

Ronaldo makes a move towards the man in possession. No.2 follows his move and suddenly Ronaldo turns and makes a move into the space he has created and receives the pass from Marcelo. Benzema and Di Maria are the players who enter the box while Khedira takes up a position outside of it.

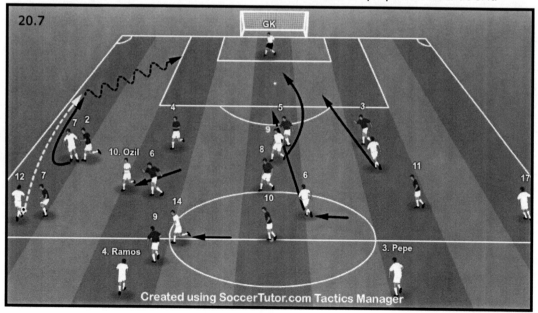

EXAMPLE 2

On diagram 20.8, Ronaldo drops back again to receive the pass from Marcelo.

As the opposition players did not shift across to the left side, there is available space around the ball zone. Marcelo passes and moves to receive towards the centre.

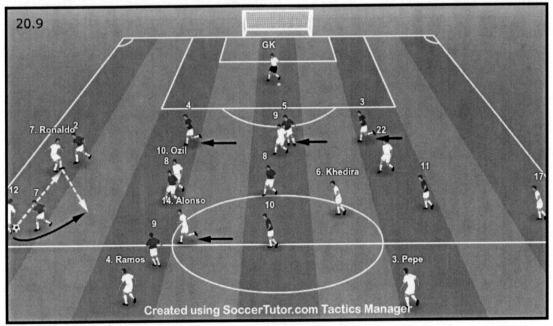

Marcelo exploits the space by making a driving run towards the opposition's goal. Ronaldo (option 1 and Benzema (option 2) move towards the free space and provide options for a final pass.

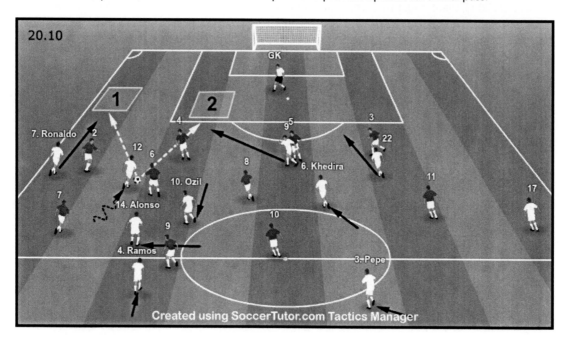

EXAMPLE 3

On diagram 20.11, there is again available space around the ball zone. Ronaldo makes a move to receive.

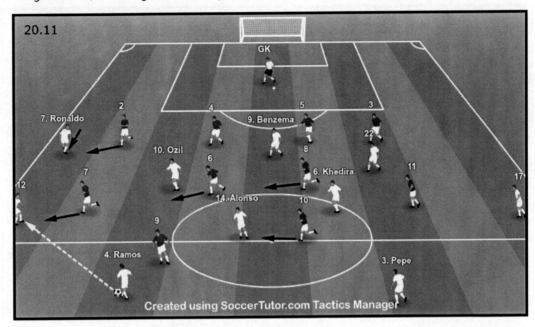

Marcelo passes the ball to Ronaldo and makes an overlapping run. Ronaldo drives the ball towards the centre and passes to Ozil. Ozil makes a first time pass to Marcelo who moves into an advanced position on the flank.

EXAMPLE 4

On diagram 20.13, Ozil drops deep to receive and No.6 follows him. This movement creates space for Ronaldo to exploit. Benzema moves towards the ball zone to provide support in front of the man in possession.

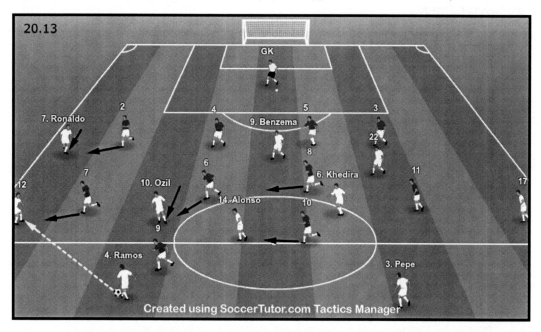

On diagram 20.14, Ronaldo dribbles with the ball and Marcelo (option 1) makes an overlapping run and Benzema (option 2) makes a diagonal run to receive a final pass behind the defensive line.

EXAMPLE 5

On diagram 20.15, we show another way Real Madrid dealt with the same tactical situation. Ronaldo again drives the ball towards the centre. Benzema drops back this time and provides support for a square pass to be made.

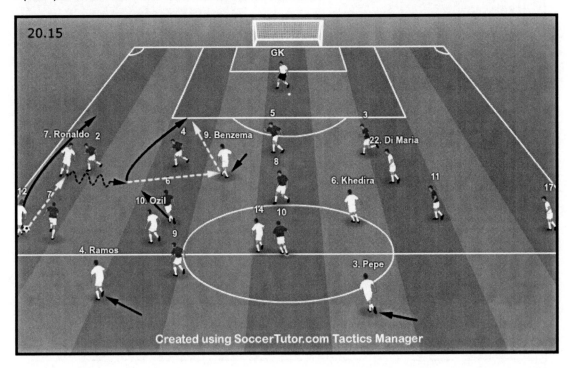

SWITCHING PLAY TO THE RIGHT FLANK

On diagram 20.16, the opposing team shifts towards the left side retaining a very compact formation which restricts the available space for Real near the ball zone. Ozil drops deep to receive and Benzema moves towards the left.

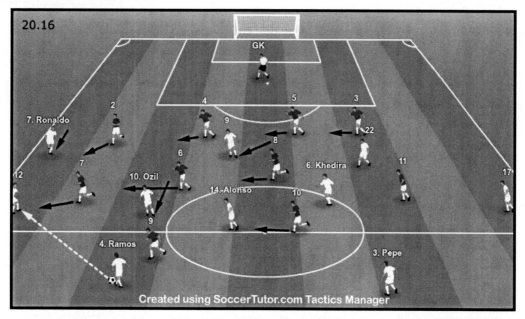

When the ball is passed to Ronaldo he is being triple marked. Ozil provides support for a backwards pass. When he receives, Ozil has 4 available passing options.

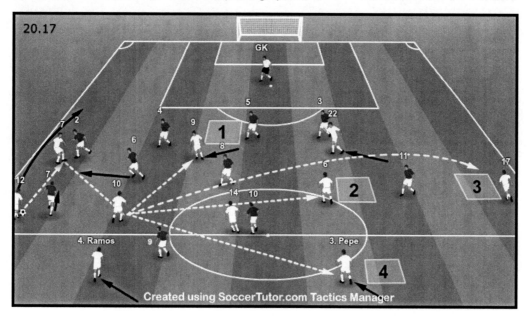

EXAMPLE 2

On diagram 20.18, the opposition retains their compactness with a collective shift and towards the left. Alonso reacts quickly, shifting across to provide support and receive a pass in the centre.

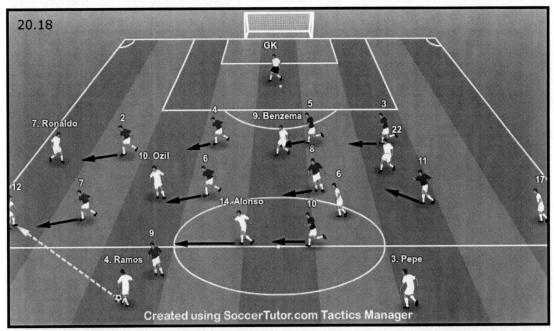

After receiving the ball, there are 4 available passing options for Alonso. The pass towards Benzema can lead to the third stage of the build up play.

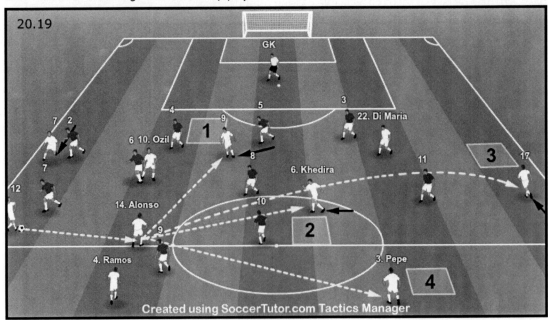

EXAMPLE 3

The situation presented on diagram 20.19 was played differently. Ozil drops deep and receives the pass from Marcelo. Alonso also moves deeper to provide a passing option for him. There are 4 available passing options for the new man in possession.

RONALDO'S DRIVING RUNS FROM THE LEFT

On diagram 20.21, No.7 of the opposition is positioned in such a way which blocks a potential vertical pass to Ronaldo. Ozil is too far away to provide a passing option.

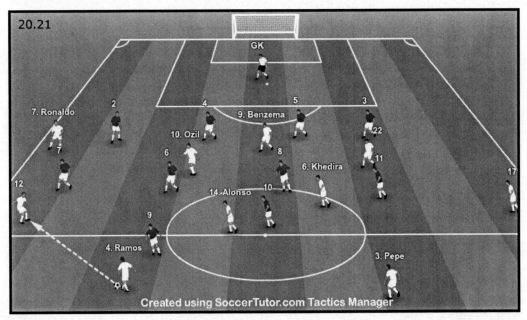

Ronaldo comes inside and receives the diagonal pass and continues his run with the ball towards the opposition's goal. Ozil moves in behind No.2 providing a passing option (option 1). Benzema (option 2) and Di Maria move to provide passing options and Ronaldo can also take a shot on goal (option 3).

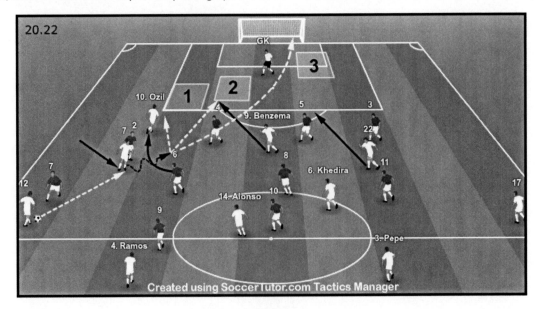

 # ASSESSMENT:

When the Real Madrid players had this positioning, the opposition would have to stretch their shape in order to mark them. This situation created space near the ball zone and made it easy for Real to break down the defence.

When the opposition retained its compactness and restricted the available space with a well timed and synchronised shift, Madrid would seek to use the width created by either playing out an attacking move on the strong side or by switching the play towards the free space on the weak side of the opposition.

ATTACKING MIDFIELDER RECEIVING VERTICAL PASSES FROM CENTRAL DEFENDERS

On diagram 20.23, Ozil manages to receive behind the opposition's midfield line. However, 2 players move quickly to double mark him.

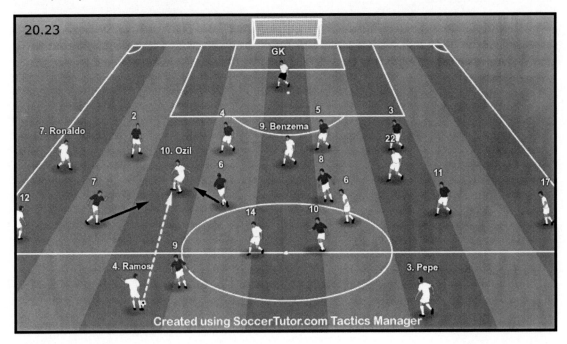

Ozil plays a first time pass to Marcelo on the left where there is available space made by Ronaldo's movement. Alonso moves towards the strong side to provide support.

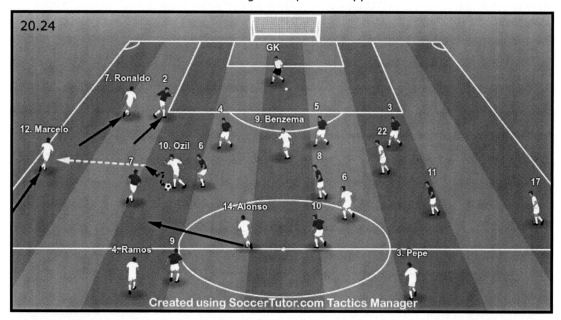

Marcelo exploits the free space and dribbles towards the penalty area. There is an available passing option towards Ronaldo (option 1) and Benzema can provide 2 options for Marcelo. He can move diagonally to receive the final pass (option 2) or he can provide support for a square pass (option 3).

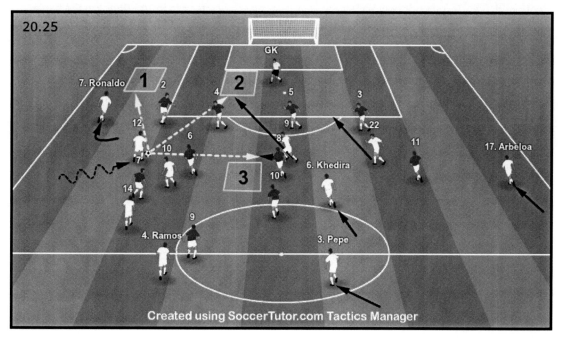

EXAMPLE 2

On diagram 20.26, Ozil makes a first time pass to Ronaldo who has made a run in behind the right back (No.2).

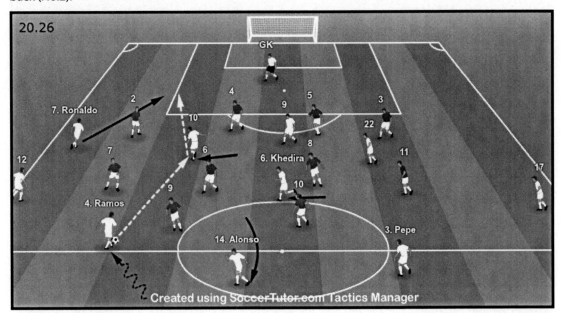

In a similar situation to the previous one, No.2 moves to block the passing lane towards Ronaldo. Ozil then takes advantage of the free space created by dribbling the ball towards the left. As already mentioned, Ozil, despite not being a very quick player was very effective in 1v1 duels on the flank.

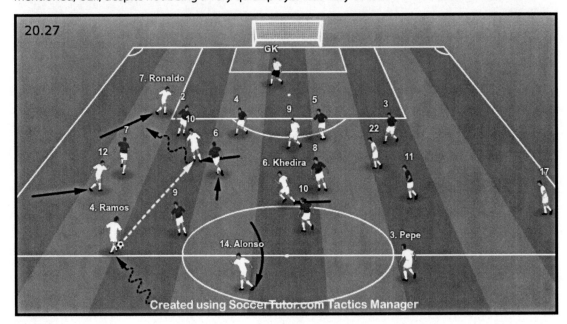

EXAMPLE 3

On diagram 20.28, the pass is directed to Ozil who is placed in between the opposition's 2 lines.

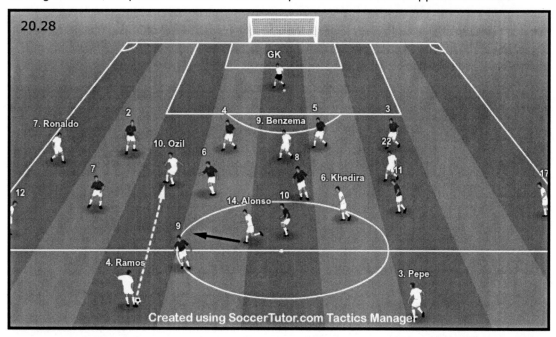

Ronaldo makes one of his favourite moves here to get free of marking and receives the ball unmarked down the flank. Ozil then moves towards the sideline to help outnumber the opposition. Ronaldo passes to Ozil who has plenty of space to exploit and get the cross in.

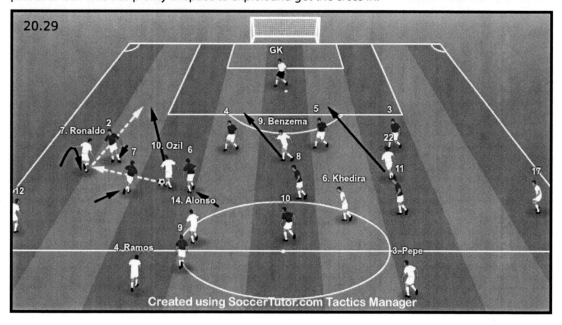

The same situation can develop in a different way with it all depending on the way No.2 deals with Ronaldo's movement.

The pass back towards Ozil is blocked, but there is space for a driving run towards the inside. So Ronaldo takes the chance and moves towards the opposition's goal. After dribbling the ball for a few of yards he is able to make a pass towards Ozil (option 1), Benzema (option 2) or even shoot on goal using his preferred right foot (option 3).

EXAMPLE 4

On diagram 20.31, Ozil receives with the opportunity to turn inside and run at the back 4 facing the opposition's goal.

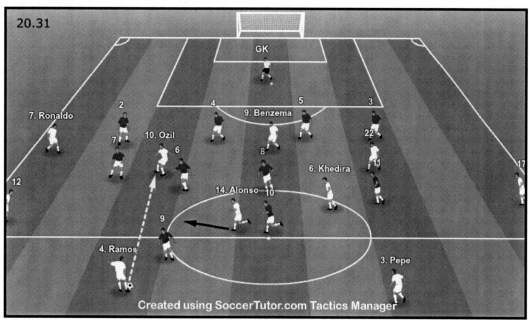

After Ozil's first touch towards the inside, Benzema (option 1) and Di Maria make diagonal moves towards the opposition's goal. The ball to Di Maria could be played in 2 ways; the diagonal pass (option 2) or the square pass (option 3).

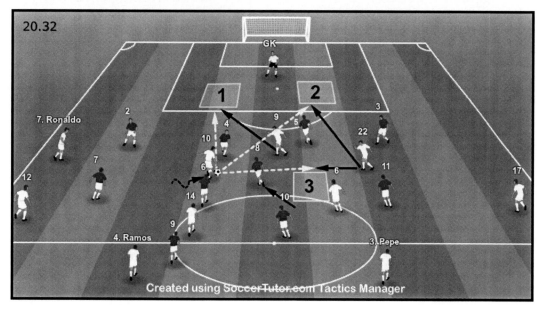

ATTACKING MIDFIELDER: DROPPING DEEP TO RECEIVE

On diagram 20.33, Ozil sees there is no passing lane which will enable him to receive behind the opposition's midfielders. So this time he drops back to provide a passing option for the man in possession in front of the opposition's midfield line.

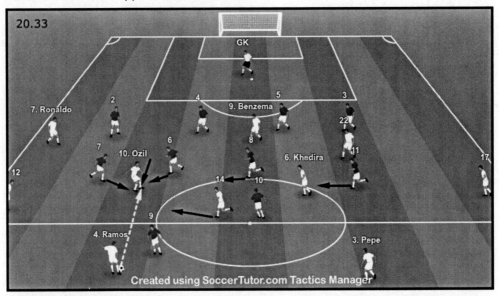

This time Ozil does not have available space to turn after receiving so passes to Alonso. As the opposing team has restricted the available space in the central zone, plenty of space is created near the sidelines. Alonso has 2 passing options (back to Pepe or a long pass to Arbeloa).

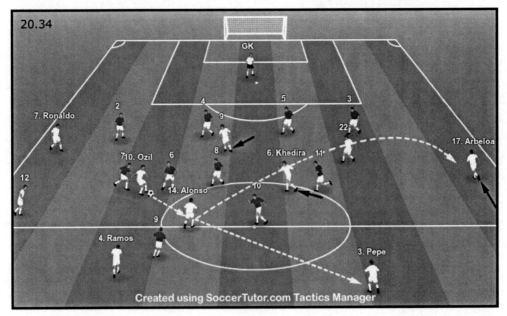

 ASSESSMENT:

Ozil used to take up positions between the defensive line and the midfield line of the opposition. He would tend to move towards the available passing lanes in order to receive the ball from the defenders or the defensive midfielders. His outstanding first touch on the ball and his awareness of his available options enabled him to fully exploit this created space without any hesitation.

When Ozil received the ball and had the chance to turn and move towards the inside of the field, the final pass was easy for him. If he received and moved towards the sideline, he used to flourish in 1v1 situations down the flank. Ozil was very effective in duels despite not being very fast.

When Ozil felt that there were no available passing lanes to receive behind the opposition's midfielders, he used to drop deep and receive in front of them.

STARTING THE BUILD UP ON THE RIGHT WITH BOTH THE WINGER AND THE FULL BACK CREATING WIDTH

When both the full back and the winger were positioned near to the sideline, the correct shape was created by the centre forward dropping deep or by Ozil's move towards the strong side.

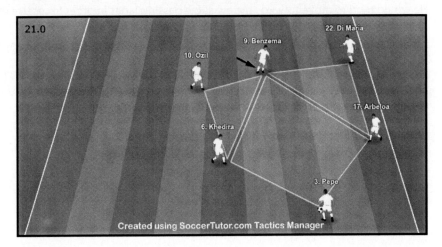

On diagrams 21.0 and 21.1, Di Maria and Arbeloa take up positions near to the sideline. Real create the correct shape with either the centre forward dropping deep or Ozil's shift towards the right at the top of the rhombus shape.

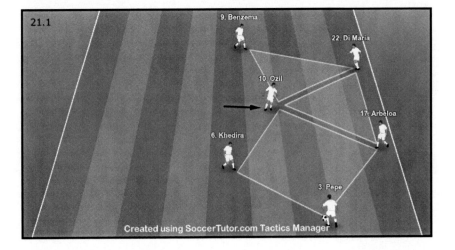

Di Maria moves back and towards the inside. With this movement he creates space on the flank. Benzema moves into the space and receives the pass from Arbeloa.

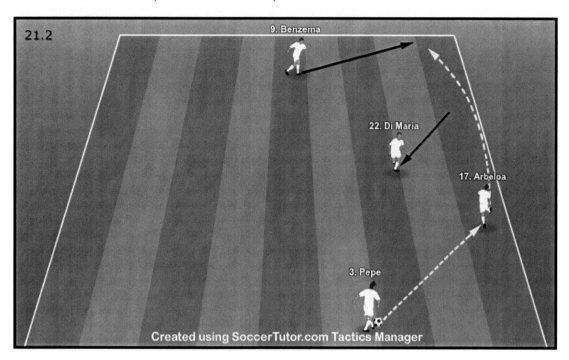

On diagram 21.3, Ozil drops back, receives and passes to Khedira. This enables the team to switch the play.

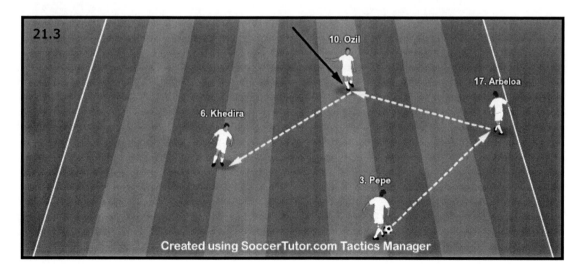

WINGERS MOVEMENT INSIDE WITHOUT THE BALL

On diagram 21.4, the first pass is to Arbeloa. Di Maria drops back to receive and create space for Benzema on the flank.

No.3 follows Di Maria. Benzema exploits the available space and receives the pass from Arbeloa.

Benzema wins the 1v1 on the flank and gets a cross into the box targeting Ronaldo and Ozil (option 1). He can also pass the ball towards Di Maria on the edge of the penalty area (option 2).

We can also see the movements of all the players who are preparing for the negative transition.

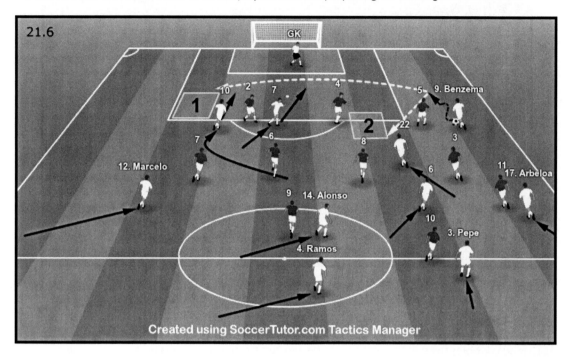

EXAMPLE 2

On diagram 21.7, we have a similar situation to the previous one.

This time the left back (No.3) does not follow Di Maria's movement so there is no space available for Benzema down the flank. Di Maria instead has the chance to receive unmarked and dribble the ball towards the centre before No.3 is able to contest him.

As Di Maria dribbles the ball towards the inside, Benzema (option 1) opens up and Ozil (option 2) makes a diagonal run. Di Maria can pass to either of them or use an in swinging cross towards Ronaldo (option 3), who has moved in between the 2 opposition defenders.

LIMITED SPACE IN BETWEEN THE MIDFIELD AND DEFENSIVE LINES

On diagram 21.9, as the opposition restricts the available space between the lines, Benzema drops deep to receive a pass from Arbeloa.

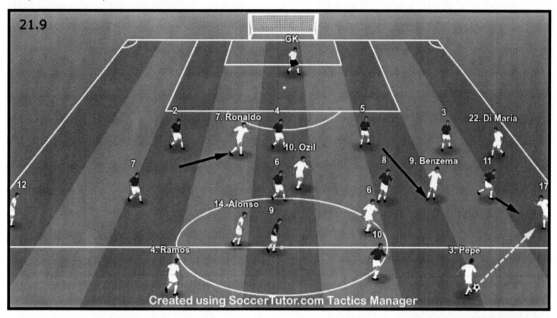

Benzema receives and passes immediately to Khedira. The new ball carrier has 4 available passing options.

EXAMPLE 2

On diagram 21.11, the opposing team is once again very compact and leaves no available space around the ball zone. Benzema again makes a move to provide support and Khedira does too.

This time the pass is made towards Khedira. As Ozil drops deep to receive, the man in possession has 3 available passing options to switch the play.

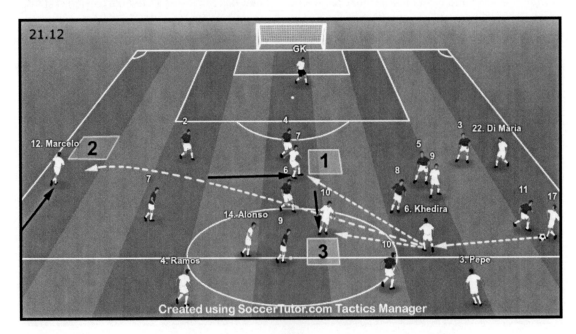

EXAMPLE 3

On diagram 21.13, Ozil is closer than Benzema to the strong side and makes a move to provide support.

As No.8 follows Ozil's movement, a gap is created in midfield. As soon as Khedira receives the pass from Arbeloa, he passes the ball to Benzema.

Benzema dribbles the ball towards the right and makes a diagonal pass to Di Maria who makes a move in behind No.3. Ronaldo enters the box ready for a potential cross. The rest of the players move up to keep the team compact and to prepare for the negative transition

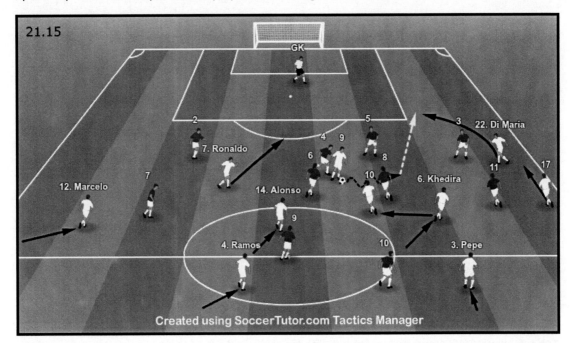

FULL BACK'S ADVANCING RUN

On diagram 21.16, we present how the situation developed if No.5 and No.3 blocked off the passing lane towards Di Maria. This time Arbeloa receives the ball and is in a position to cross the ball into the penalty area. As both the winger and the full back are in advanced positions, Khedira moves to provide cover towards the right.

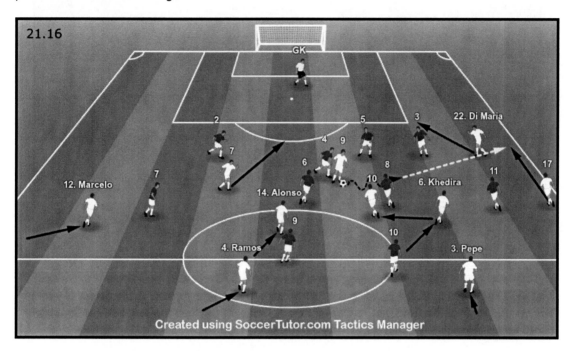

RECEIVING IN THE 'PASSING LANE'

On diagram 21.17, Ronaldo makes a move into the available passing lane between the opposition's midfielders. No.2 does not follow him as he tries to retain a balanced position as Marcelo moves forward.

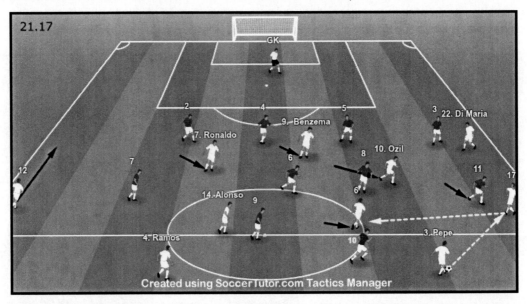

Ronaldo receives the ball free of marking and dribbles towards the centre. No.2 decides to contest him but Ronaldo has 3 passing options; the vertical pass to Benzema (option 1), the diagonal pass to Di Maria (option 2) or the short pass to Ozil (option 3). Option 3 can lead to a one-two combination. Alonso moves forward to provide support and is the safety player.

SWITCHING PLAY TO THE LEFT FLANK

On diagram 21.19, Ronaldo drops deep again to receive, but this time No.2 follows his movement.
Space is created for Marcelo to receive down the flank completely unmarked.

Marcelo receives and 4 Madrid players move into or just outside the box to receive the potential out
swinging cross. Alonso moves to provide cover for both the full back and the winger.

RIGHT WINGER'S INSIDE RUNS

On diagram 21.21, Benzema drops deep, receives and passes to Di Maria on the flank.

Benzema makes a run inside towards the opposition left back to create space for Ozil and Di Maria. Di Maria takes advantage of the created space and dribbles the ball towards the centre.

Di Maria targets Ronaldo (who moves into the penalty area) with an in swinging cross. Khedira and Arbeloa are the safety players in this situation.

EXAMPLE 2

On diagram 21.24, there is an attempt from Real to outnumber the opposition on the right side. Kaka moves towards the available passing lane and receives behind the opposition's midfielders. He has enough time and space to turn as No.5 and No.3 both have direct opponents to mark so are unable to move forward and contest Kaka.

Kaka passes the ball to Di Maria and runs in behind to help outnumber the opposition down the flank and create space for the ball carrier. Ronaldo and Higuain take up positions ready for the potential cross.

No.3 blocks the pass towards Kaka but leaves space towards the inside of the field. Di Maria dribbles the ball towards the centre and crosses for Ronaldo and Higuain. Arbeloa and Khedira are the safety players. The rest of the Real Madrid players take up positions preparing for the potential negative transition.

STARTING THE BUILD UP ON THE LEFT WITH THE WIDTH CREATED BY THE WINGER

When the width on the left was provided by the winger, the rhombus shape was created by Ronaldo, Ozil and with Benzema at the top. Marcelo was the player at the base of the shape. This shape was mainly created when switching play from the right to the left side.

On diagram 22.0, Marcelo takes up a position towards the centre and Ronaldo is near to the sideline. In this situation, Alonso has the chance to move higher up the pitch because Marcelo is in a position which enables him to cover the holding midfielder's advanced position.

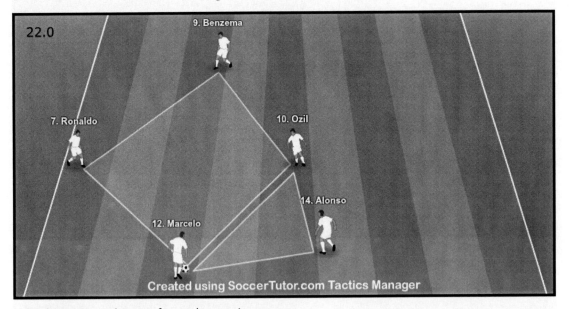

Marcelo passes and moves forward to receive.

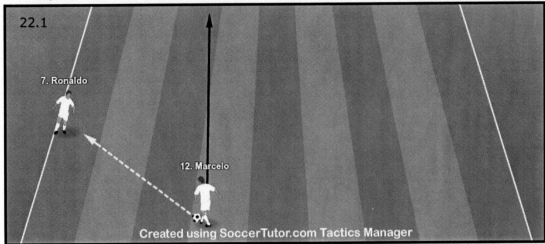

Marcelo passes the ball to Ronaldo again and as Ronaldo dribbles the ball towards the centre, Marcelo makes an overlapping run.

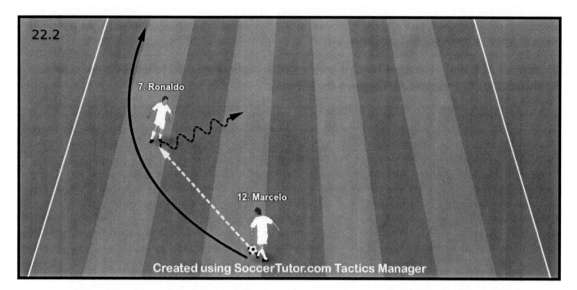

Ronaldo works in collaboration with Higuain as he passes the ball to him and makes a move to receive the pass back towards the inside.

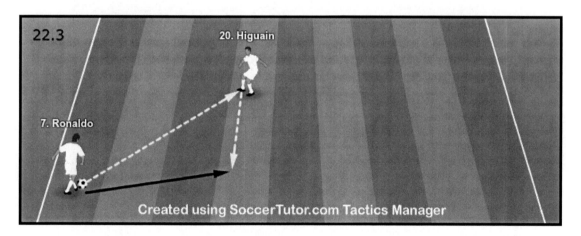

SWITCHING PLAY FROM THE RIGHT TO THE LEFT

The diagrams to follow present how the Real Madrid players switched the play from right to left. We see how they developed their attacking moves on the left using the passing combinations shown in diagrams 22.0 to 22.3 on the previous pages.

On diagram 22.4, the ball reaches Marcelo after a switch of play from right to left. Both the opposing team and all the Real players shift towards the left side.

Marcelo passes to Ronaldo and then makes an inside run which helps outnumber the opposition on the flank. Alonso moves to provide safety and Benzema drops a few yards back providing a passing option as well as dragging No.4 out of position and enables Marcelo to receive unmarked.

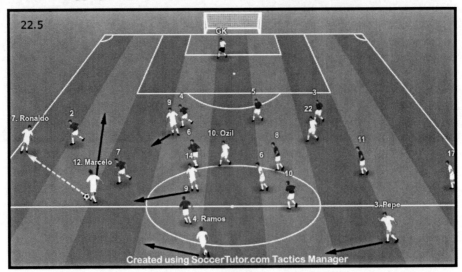

FULL BACK'S OVERLAPPING RUNS ON THE FLANK

The pass is made towards Marcelo in behind the defence on the flank.

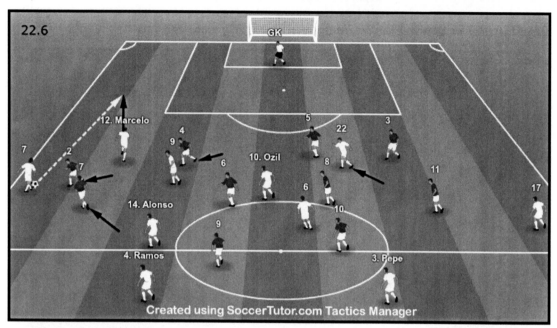

Marcelo puts a cross into the box for Di Maria and Ozil. Benzema moves to a position just outside the box and Ronaldo into a position which enables him to receive a pass back. Alonso shifts towards the left to provide safety. The rest of the Madrid players move to prepare for the negative transition.

DIAGONAL RUNS IN BEHIND THE DEFENSIVE LINE

Here we have a similar situation to the previous one. After Marcelo passes to Ronaldo he moves forward and Benzema drops back to receive. This time No.4 reacts to Marcelo's movement and shifts across to mark him. However, this means that Benzema is now unmarked.

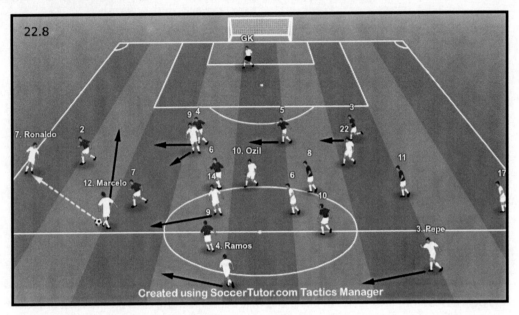

As soon as Benzema receives, he has the chance to turn towards the opposition's goal and pass to either Di Maria (option 1) who makes a diagonal run or to Ozil (option 2) who takes advantage of the free space Di Maria has created.

THE FULL BACK CREATING SPACE FOR THE WINGER

On diagram 22.10, Ronaldo receives and dribbles the ball towards the centre.

Marcelo makes an overlapping run creating a 2v1 situation on the flank. Benzema makes a move to receive as well as to create space for Ozil. Ronaldo can pass to either Marcelo (option 1) or to Ozil (option 2).

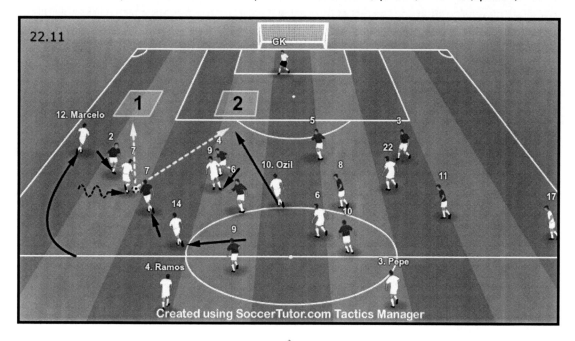

ONE TOUCH COMBINATION PLAY ON THE LEFT

On diagram 22.12, as soon as Ronaldo receives, he is under pressure from No.2. Benzema exploits the free space in behind No.2. As the pressure from No.2 prevents the ball carrier from making a driving run towards the inside, he passes the ball to Benzema, moves towards the inside and receives the back pass.

Ronaldo, after driving the ball towards the opposition's goal, has the chance to pass to Benzema on the left (option 1) or have a one–two combination with Ozil (option 2). Both Marcelo and Alonso move to a safety player's position and the rest of the Real players move to positions which will enable them to react effectively in case possession is lost

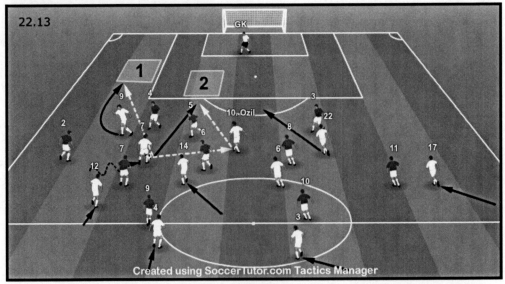

EXAMPLE 2

On diagram 22.14, Ronaldo receives the ball and Benzema moves across to provide support.

Ronaldo combines with Benzema and receives the pass back from him.

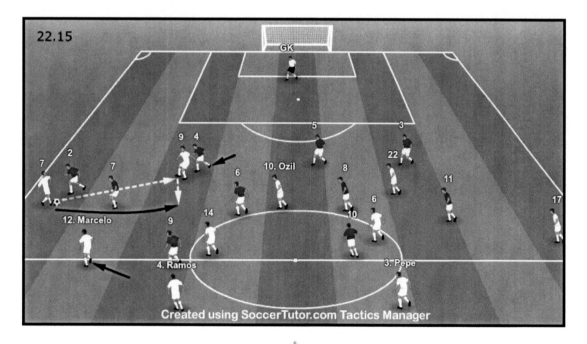

RONALDO'S FINAL PASS IN BEHIND THE DEFENCE

Ronaldo dribbles the ball towards the inside and has 2 passing options. He can pass to Benzema (option 1) who opens up on the left or to Di Maria (option 2) who makes a diagonal run.

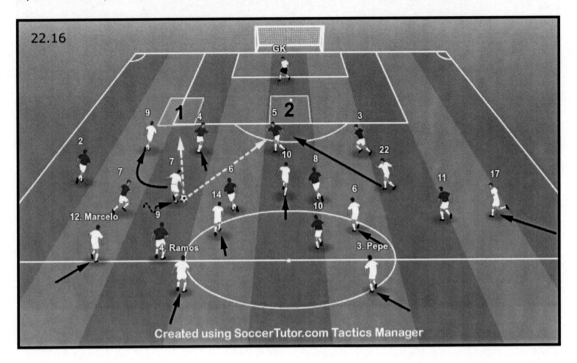

STARTING THE BUILD UP ON THE RIGHT WITH THE WIDTH CREATED BY THE WINGER

On diagram 22.17, Arbeloa is placed towards the centre and Di Maria

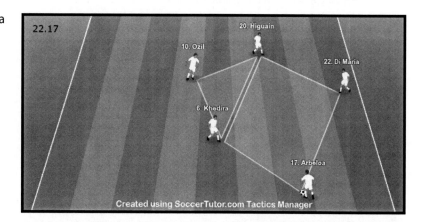

Arbeloa passes to Di Maria and as he dribbles the ball towards the centre, Arbeloa makes an overlapping run.

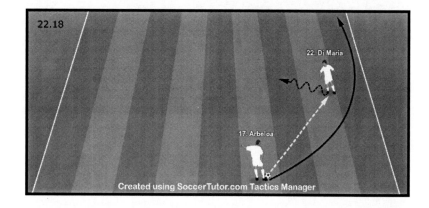

Arbeloa passes to Di Maria who has moved back to receive. After passing the ball, Arbeloa moves forward.

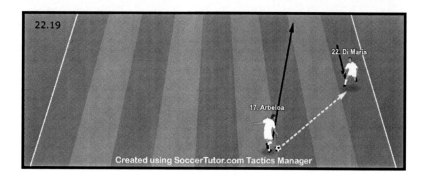

THE RIGHT WINGER RECEIVING THE BALL DEEP ON THE FLANK

On diagram 22.20, Real move the ball from the left to the right. Both sets of players shift towards the right. Di Maria is placed near to the sideline and provides width.

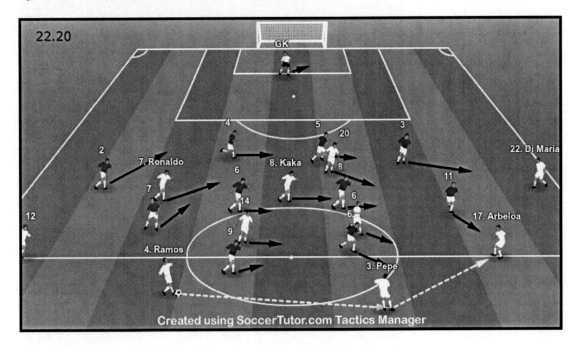

On diagram 22.21, the pass is made towards Di Maria. After passing the ball, Arbeloa makes an inside run to outnumber the opposition left back on the flank and creates space for the new ball carrier.

Due to the opposition's poor defensive reaction, Di Maria is able to pass the ball to Arbeloa who moves forward with the ball and crosses into the box targeting Ronaldo and Higuain. Kaka and Di Maria move to positions outside the box. Khedira is the safety player.

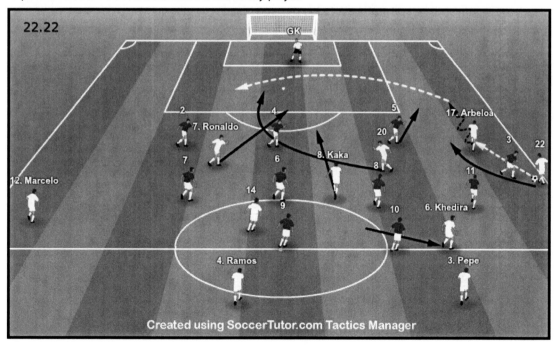

EXAMPLE 2

On diagram 22.23, Arbeloa passes and makes the same move again to create superiority in numbers down the flank. Higuain moves to provide support.

As No.3 contests Di Maria in such a way that the ball can not be passed directly to Arbeloa, Di Maria passes to Higuain and the ball reaches Arbeloa through him.

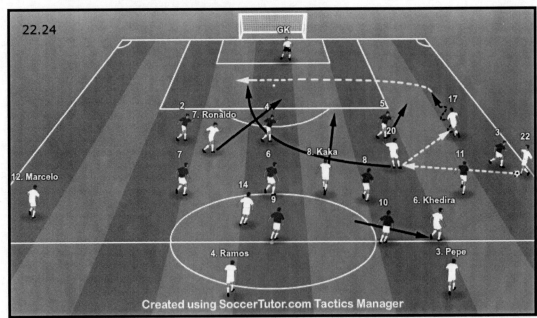

EXAMPLE 3

On diagram 22.25, there is a similar situation to the previous one. This time the opposition's left winger (No.11) tracks Arbeloa's forward run.

Di Maria exploits the free space Arbeloa creates and dribbles the ball towards the centre. Higuain opens up to receive (option 1) and Ronaldo makes a diagonal run (option 2). Kaka provides one more passing option (3) towards the centre of the field with a potential one-two combination. Khedira is the safety man for Real Madrid.

EXAMPLE 4

On diagram 22.27, Arbeloa passes to Di Maria and makes an overlapping run which again leads to outnumbering the opposition on the flank.

As the opposition does not have an effective defensive reaction and the opposition's winger (No.11) did not manage to close down the ball carrier in time, Di Maria finds space towards the centre and converges. Higuain who opens up (option 1) and Ronaldo (option 2) who moves diagonally provide passing options. Khedira again moves towards the right to provide safety.

EXAMPLE 5

On diagram 22.29, Arbeloa passes and again makes an overlapping run. No.11 follows his movement.

This time the opposition has dealt well with Real's attempt to outnumber them down the flank. So the team seeks to move the ball to the weak side by passing the ball to Khedira who is in a supporting position and then to Marcelo (option 2). Kaka also provides a passing option (option between the opposition's lines.

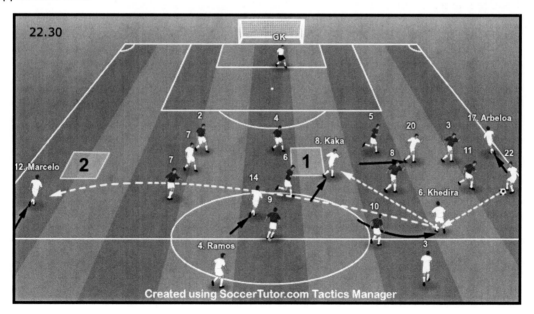

EXAMPLE 4

On diagram 22.31, Arbeloa passes the ball and then stays in a supporting position behind Di Maria. Higuain tries to exploit the free space behind No.3 and creates space for the new man in possession at the same time.

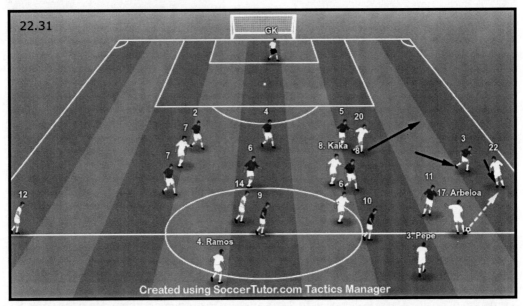

The left back's (No.3) positioning prevents Di Maria from passing the ball to Higuain, but leaves enough free space to dribble the ball towards the centre. Kaka takes advantage of the space created by Higuain and moves to receive (option 1). Ronaldo also makes a diagonal run between the right back and the central defender to receive a potential in swinging cross (option 2).

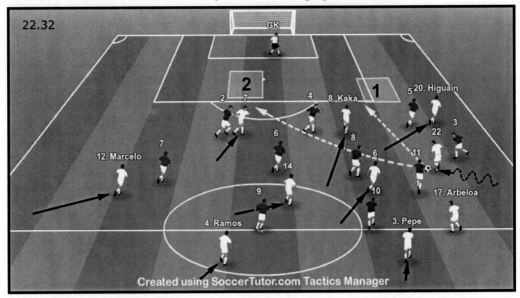

CHAPTER 5

COMBINATIONS AFTER A LONG PASS TOWARDS THE WEAK SIDE OF THE OPPOSITION

THE LONG PASS IS DIRECTED TOWARDS THE LEFT SIDE AND THE FULL BACK PROVIDES WIDTH

Real Madrid frequently used long passes towards the weak side of the opposing team so they could exploit the free space down the flanks. This usually happened when the opposition squeezed the available space in the central zone to prevent Real from attacking through the middle. The combinations that were used most often in these situations are presented in the diagrams to follow. In the situation on diagram 23.0, Marcelo receives the long pass from Pepe. Ronaldo moves to provide support in front of him. Marcelo passes to Ronaldo and moves to receive the pass back on the inside.

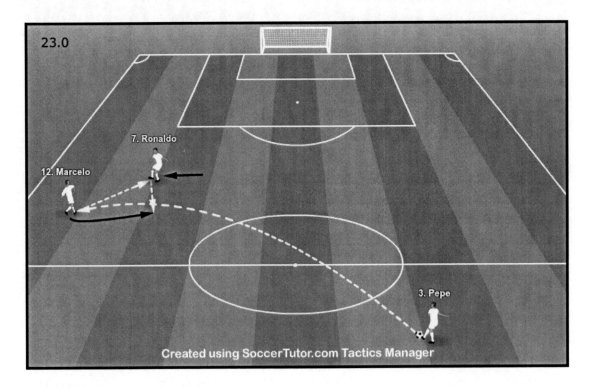

On diagram 23.1, Ronaldo drops back and receives the ball in a deep position.

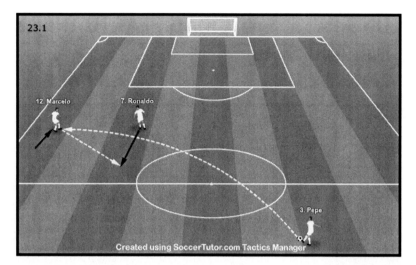

On diagram 23.2, Ronaldo and Marcelo move in opposite directions. By carrying out this action, Ronaldo creates space for Real's left back and enables him to receive in an advanced position.

In a similar situation to the previous one, Ronaldo moves towards the centre to provide a passing option for Alonso. At the same time, he creates space on the flank for Marcelo to run into as he receives the ball in an advanced position

LONG PASS: SWITCHING PLAY TO THE LEFT BACK WITH TIME AND SPACE

On diagram 23.4, the long pass is made by Pepe to Marcelo.

Marcelo moves forward as the opposing team shifts towards the left side and retains its balance. The opposition winger (No.7) moves to close Marcelo down and No.2 is in a covering position. Ronaldo drops deep to receive unmarked and Alonso takes up a position which provides safety.

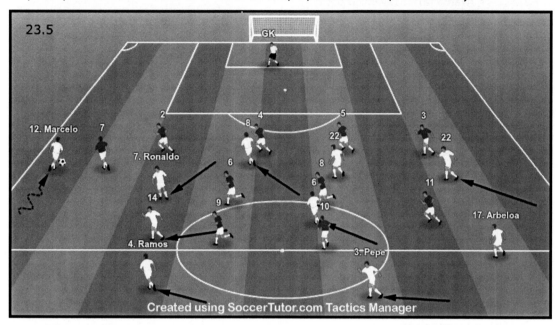

As soon as Ronaldo receives, he has 2 passing options. Higuain and Di Maria make diagonal runs to receive a potential in swinging cross (option 2). Kaka is in a position to receive a short pass (option 1) and turn towards the opposition's goal

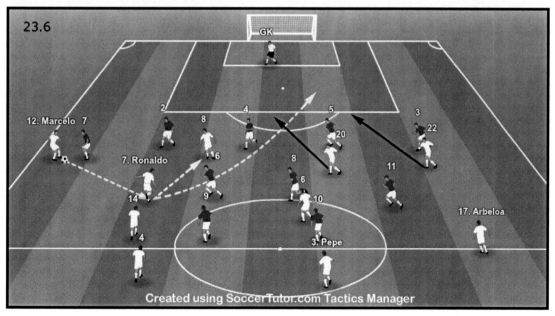

EXAMPLE 2

On diagram 23.7, Ronaldo moves towards Khedira to receive and creates space for Marcelo to exploit as he moves forward into an advanced position.

Marcelo crosses the ball into the box targeting Higuain and Kaka. Ronaldo moves to a position just outside the box and Alonso shifts towards the left to provide safety.

EXAMPLE 3

On diagram 23.9, Ronaldo drops deep again to receive and create space on the flank.

No.2 does not follow Ronaldo's movement and remains in a good defensive position. He drops back and waits for No.7 to close Marcelo down. Ronaldo moves into the passing lane between No.2 and No.7 and receives. He has 2 passing options; a diagonal pass to Higuain (option 1) and a short pass to Kaka (option 2) which can lead to a one–two combination.

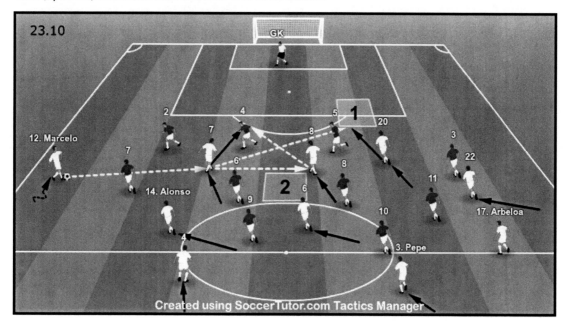

EXAMPLE 4

In a similar situation to the previous one, Marcelo receives the ball wide on the left.

Marcelo passes to Ronaldo and moves to receive the pass back. Ronaldo makes this pass as he is unable to turn towards the opposition's goal due to the heavy pressure from No. 4.

Marcelo receives the ball from Ronaldo and has 3 passing options in behind the defensive line. He can pass to Ronaldo (option 1), to Kaka (option 2) who takes advantage of the free space in the centre of defence and to Higuain (option 3) who makes a diagonal run. Alonso is the safety player

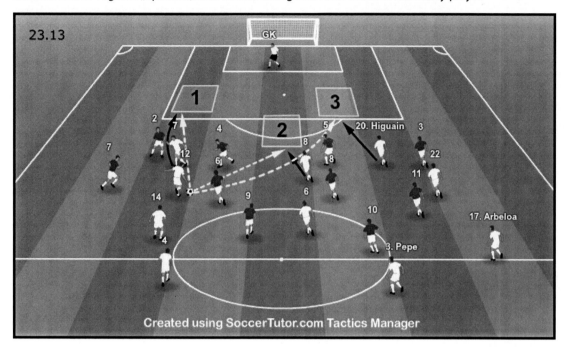

EXAMPLE 5

On diagram 23.14, Ronaldo drops back to receive and No.7 moves to block the potential pass to him.

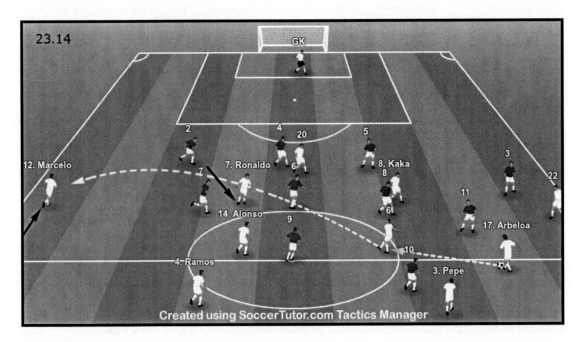

Marcelo receives and moves towards the centre with the ball. Higuain (option 1) moves diagonally behind the defensive line and Kaka (option 2) between the lines in order to receive a potential pass.

ASSESSMENT:

When Marcelo and Ronaldo were in the positions presented diagrams (23.4 - 23.15). Marcelo received the ball in a deep and wide position, Ronaldo rarely made a move towards the sideline to receive. He preferred to provide support by staying in his favoured position towards the centre.

THE LONG PASS IS DIRECTED TOWARDS THE LEFT AND THE WINGER PROVIDES THE WIDTH

When Real Madrid switched the play using a long pass towards the weak side and the winger was the player who provided width, the team used certain combinations in order to break through the opposition's defence. These combinations are presented in the diagrams to follow.

On diagram 24.0, Pepe makes a long pass to Ronaldo who is placed near to the sideline and creating width. Marcelo used to make runs ahead of Ronaldo to receive the ball down the flank behind the opposition's left back (option 1) or outside the penalty area (option 2).

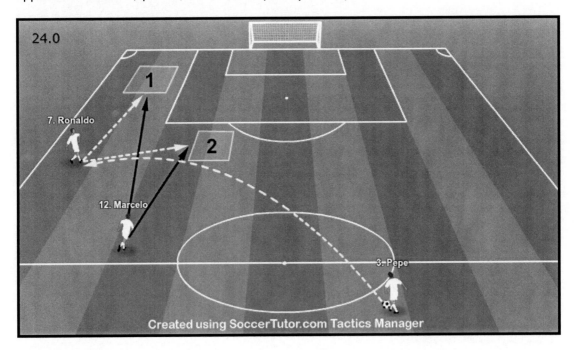

On diagram 24.1, Ronaldo receives the long pass in a wide position and dribbles the ball towards the centre. Marcelo makes an overlapping run and receives the pass on the flank.

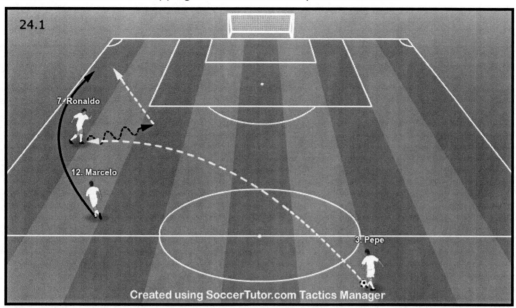

On diagram 24.2, Marcelo is too far away to move into an advanced position ahead of Ronaldo, who has possession after Pepe's long pass. This time Benzema is the player who exploits the free space behind the opposition's left back and finally receives the pass. This movement from Benzema on either flank was very frequent and he was able to play effectively as a winger too

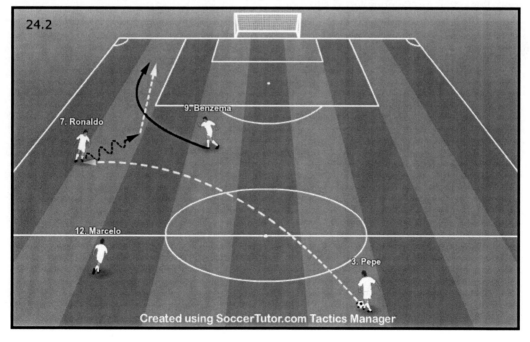

RONALDO IN SPACE ON THE LEFT FLANK

On diagram 24.3, Ronaldo receives the long ball from Pepe wide on the left.

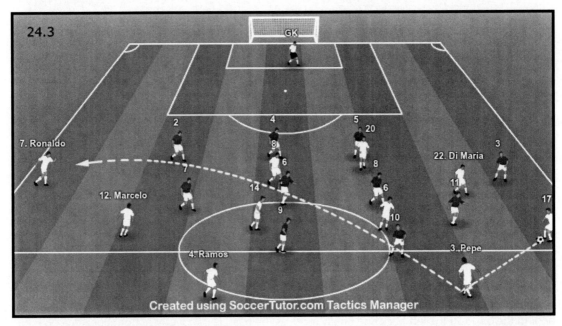

As the right winger of the opposition (No.7) is too far away from the right back (No.2) to provide support, Ronaldo is in a favourable 1v1 situation.

Ronaldo was extremely effective in these situations. After getting past No.2, he can cross into the box to target Higuain and Di Maria (option 1). He can also pass inside to Kaka (option 2).

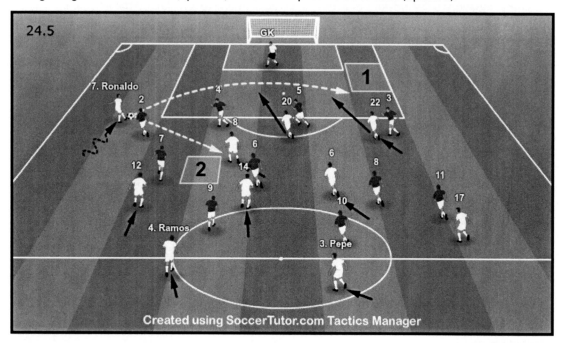

EXAMPLE 2

In a similar situation to the previous one, the pass is again made to Ronaldo on the left. flank.

Marcelo takes advantage of the transmission phase and makes an inside run in behind No.2. Ronaldo dribbles the ball towards the inside and makes a pass to meet Marcelo's run.

Marcelo can either cross the ball (option 1) or pass to the outside the box for Ronaldo (option 2). Alonso provides safety by shifting towards the left. The rest of the Real Madrid players move to prepare for the negative transition.

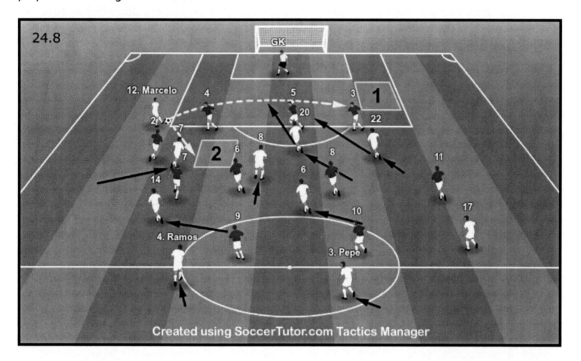

THE FULL BACK IN THE FINAL THIRD

On diagram 24.9, Ronaldo receives from Pepe again. This time Higuain is positioned towards the left and Kaka towards the right. The right winger of the opposition (No.7) has a position which enables him to move across and double mark the new ball carrier. Higuain responds by moving towards the sideline to receive and creates space at the same time.

Ronaldo passes the ball inside to Marcelo who makes a run towards the opposition's goal exploiting the free space created by Higuain. Alonso moves towards the left to provide safety.

Marcelo moves forward with the ball and can either pass to Higuain (option 1) who opens up, or to Kaka (option 2) who moves to provide support for a one-two combination.

FULL BACK'S OVERLAPPING RUN ON THE LEFT FLANK

On diagram's 24.12, we have the same situation once again with Ronaldo on the left.

Ronaldo receives and moves towards the centre as Marcelo makes an overlapping run. Higuain drops deep to receive unmarked inside. No.4 had to drop back to cover No.2's position to prevent a 2v1 situation on the flank. Ronaldo decides to pass the ball to Higuain.

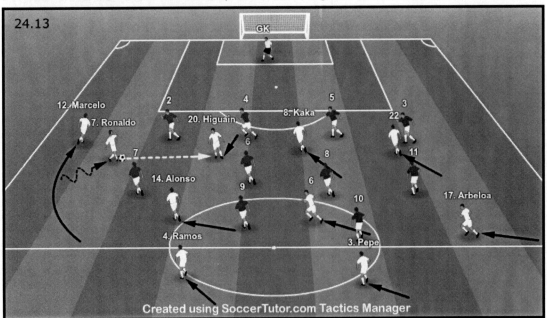

Higuain moves forward with the ball and has 3 passing options. Alonso again provides safety covering for Marcelo's forward run.

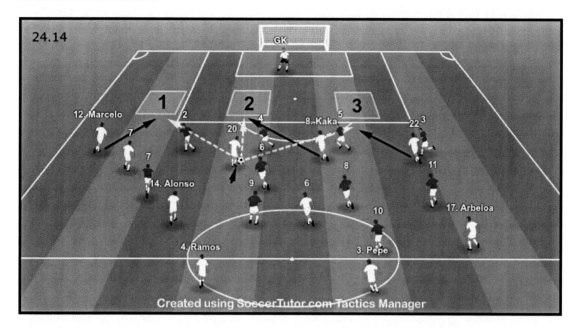

The previous situation can progress in a different way. This time No.4 steps up to mark Higuain, so Ronaldo decides to pass the ball to Marcelo. Marcelo crosses the ball towards Kaka and Di Maria in the penalty area.

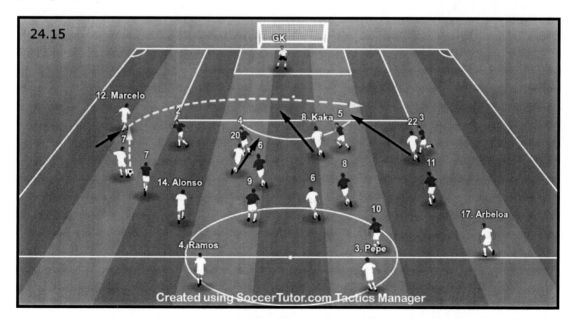

CENTRE FORWARD RUNS IN BEHIND THE RIGHT BACK

On diagram 24.16, the ball is directed to Ronaldo again. Marcelo is in a deep position so he is too far away to move into an advanced position ahead of Ronaldo. Higuain makes a run towards the flank to receive and create space.

Ronaldo dribbles the ball towards the centre taking on No.2 who is left without cover because No.4 followed Higuain's movement. Ronaldo can pass to either Higuain (option 1) or Kaka (option 2). He also has the opportunity to shoot on goal (option 3).

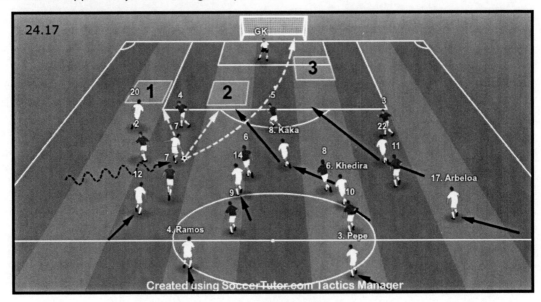

THE LONG PASS TOWARDS THE LEFT WITH BOTH THE FULL BACK AND THE WINGER PROVIDING WIDTH

When there was a switch of play towards the weak side of the opposition on the left and both the winger and the full back had wide positions, Real Madrid used the combinations which are presented in the diagrams to follow.

Diagram 25.0 presents a situation where both Ronaldo and Marcelo take up wide positions. Marcelo makes an overlapping run again and receives a pass from Ronaldo after he has carried the ball towards the centre.

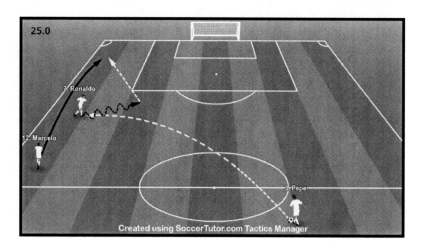

On diagram 25.1, after Ronaldo receives the ball, Marcelo moves diagonally towards the inside and to receive a pass just outside the opposition's penalty area.

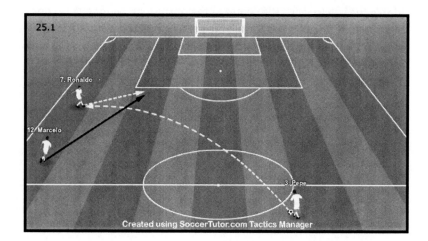

POSITIONING FOR THE NEGATIVE TRANSITION

On diagram 25.2, the ball is directed to Ronaldo on the left flank from a long pass by Pepe. Marcelo takes advantage of the transmission phase and makes an overlapping run.

No.2 takes over Marcelo's marking which leaves Ronaldo under No.7's guidance. Ronaldo is able to dribble the ball towards the centre as the opposition winger (No.7) does not manage to close him down in time. Ronaldo has 3 available passing options. Alonso moves into a position which provides safety. The rest of the players move into positions which enable the team to react successfully if possession is lost.

DIAGONAL RUNS/PASSES IN THE FINAL THIRD

On diagram 25.4, the ball is directed to Ronaldo once again, but this time the opposition's No.7 has a much better defensive position.

No.2 and No.7 move to double mark Ronaldo. Higuain moves towards the sideline to stretch the defence while Marcelo makes a run towards the centre and receives the pass from Ronaldo.

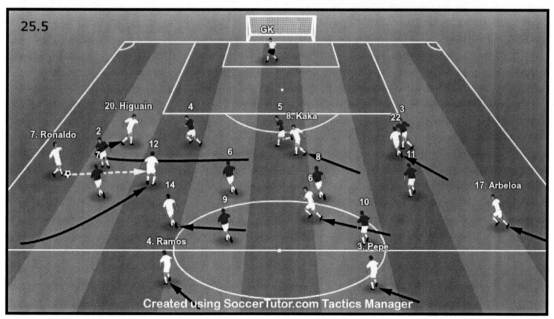

Marcelo dribbles the ball towards the opposition's goal and has 2 easy passing options in behind the defensive line.

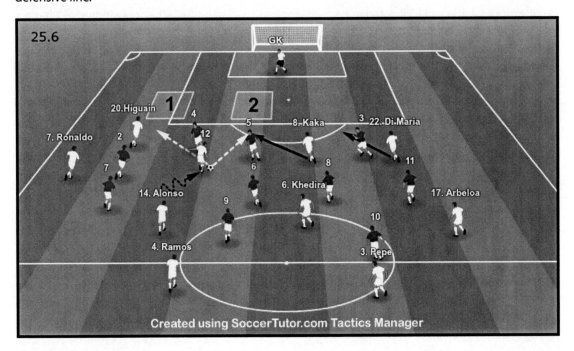

THE LONG PASS IS DIRECTED TOWARDS THE RIGHT AND THE FULL BACK PROVIDES WIDTH

When the switch of play was directed towards the right and the full back was the player who provided width, Real Madrid used the passing combinations presented in the diagrams to follow.

On diagram 26.0, the long pass is made towards the right side. Arbeloa is the player who creates width and receives. Di Maria moves down the flank to receive in the free space.

On diagram 26.1, Di Maria moves towards the man in possession to receive and also helps create space for Arbeloa. Arbeloa receives the ball in an advanced position and passes to Benzema who makes one of his usual runs towards the flank.

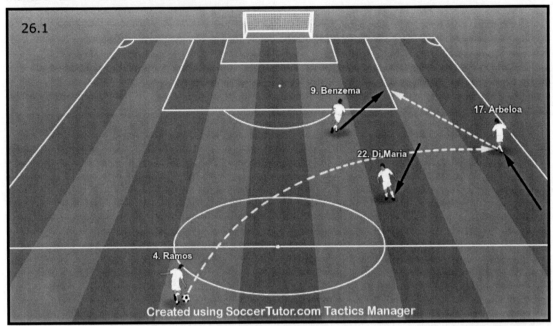

On diagram 26.2, as Arbeloa receives the long ball from Ramos, Di Maria drops back to provide support and creates space for Khedira who would often move into advanced positions exploiting the free spaces. The man in possession has 2 passing options.

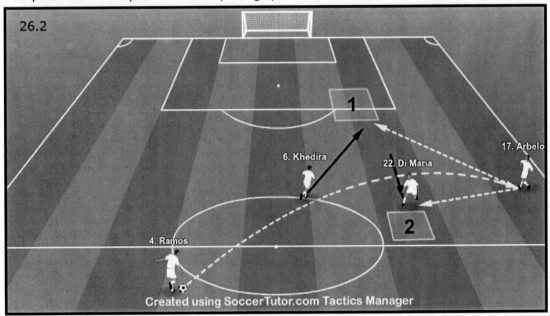

RIGHT WINGER WITH BACK TO GOAL ON THE FLANK

On diagram 26.3, there is a switch of play from the left to the right and the pass is directed to Arbeloa from Alonso. Di Maria makes a move into the free space near to the sideline.

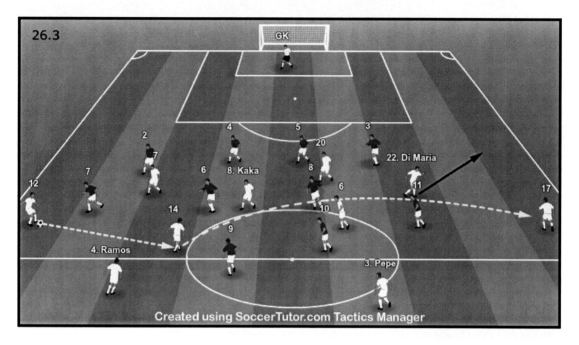

Arbeloa passes to Di Maria on the flank, as all the players move towards the weak side.

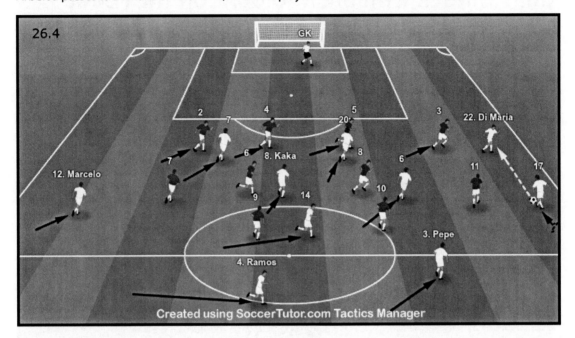

Di Maria turns with the ball and gets hits an in swinging cross towards Higuain and Ronaldo, while Khedira makes an inside run to provide another passing option.

CENTRE FORWARD RUNS IN BEHIND THE LEFT BACK

On diagram 26.6, the pass is directed towards Arbeloa and this time Di Maria drops back to receive.

Arbeloa moves forward with the ball as No.3 drops back to give No.11 the chance to close the ball carrier down.

Khedira makes an inside run behind No.3 and receives the ball. The cross into the box targets Ronaldo and Higuain. Kaka moves to a position at the edge of the penalty area.

EXAMPLE 2

On diagram 26.9, the pass is directed to Arbeloa again. Di Maria drops back and Higuain moves in behind No.3 and towards the sideline.

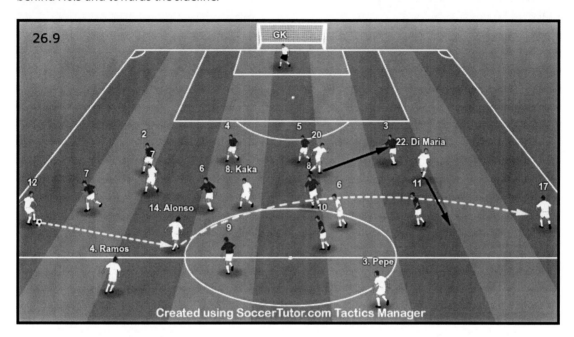

Arbeloa passes to Higuain on the right

Higuain is under No.5's pressure. Khedira makes an inside run, receives and can cross to Kaka on the far post (option 1) or Ronaldo near the penalty spot (option 2).

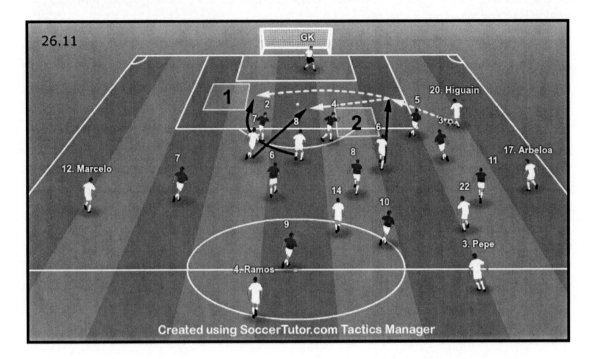

THE LONG PASS IS DIRECTED TOWARDS THE RIGHT AND THE WINGER PROVIDES WIDTH

There were times during the switch of play towards the right where the winger was the player that provided width and the full back would be placed more centrally. The diagrams to follow present some of the most frequent combinations used by the Real Madrid players in this particular tactical situation.

On diagram 27.0, Arbeloa makes an inside run behind the opposition's left back and receives the pass from Di Maria.

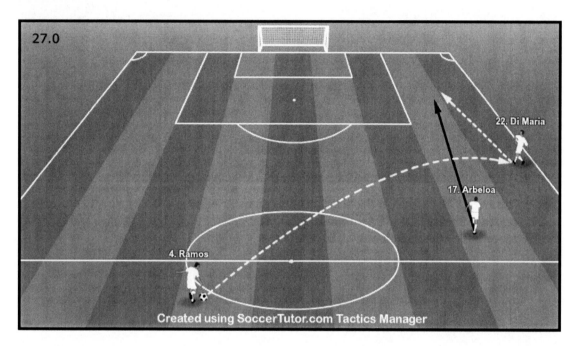

CHAPTER 5

On diagram 27.1, Di Maria receives and Arbeloa is positioned towards the centre. As Di Maria makes a driving run towards the centre, Arbeloa makes an overlapping run and receives.

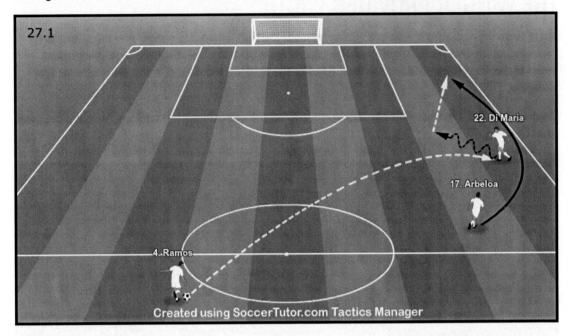

On diagram 27.2, Di Maria receives the long ball from Ramos. As Arbeloa is too far away to provide a passing option in front of Di Maria, Benzema makes the movement towards the sideline and exploits the free space behind the opposition's left back.

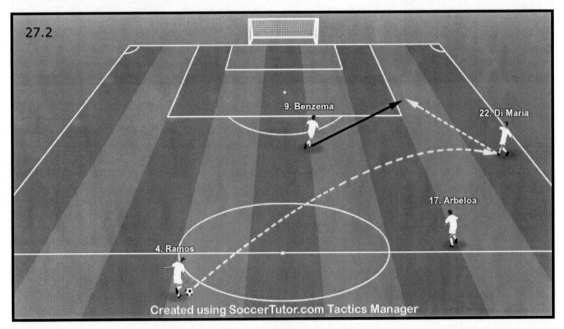

RIGHT BACK'S OVERLAPPING RUNS ON THE FLANK

On diagram 27.3, Alonso makes a long pass towards Di Maria who is positioned near the sideline. Arbeloa takes advantage of the transmission phase and makes an inside run behind No.3's back.

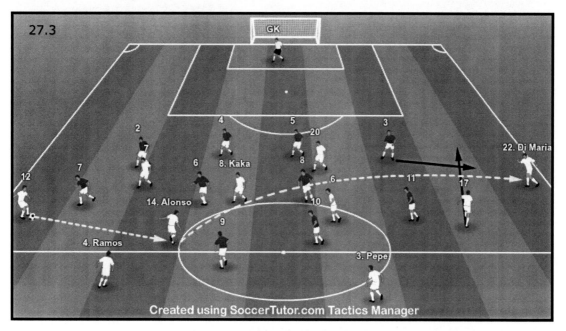

The Real Madrid players manage to outnumber the opposition on the flank and Di Maria passes the ball to Arbeloa. Khedira shifts towards the right to provide safety.

Arbeloa moves forward with the ball and can either cross into the box for Ronaldo and Higuain (option 1) or pass to Kaka on the edge of the penalty area (option 2).

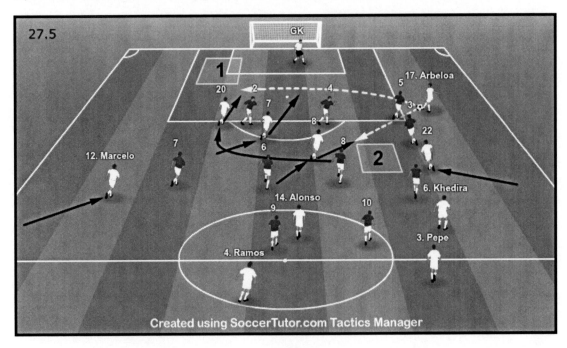

OUTNUMBERING THE OPPOSITION ON THE FLANK

On diagram 27.6 the pass is directed to Di Maria again who receives and moves inside. Arbeloa makes an overlapping run to outnumber the opposition near the sideline.

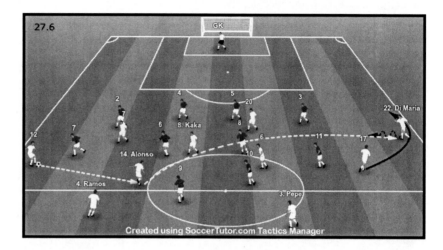

No.3 is outnumbered by Di Maria and Arbeloa. This means that the ball carrier has enough available time and space before he is closed down by No.11.

Higuain makes a diagonal run to receive a pass behind the defensive line (option 2), while Ronaldo moves between the right back and the central defender for a potential cross (option 1). Di Maria also has the chance to pass the ball to Arbeloa on the right (option 3). Khedia provides safety on the right again.

EXAMPLE 2

On diagram 27.8, Di Maria receives the long ball on the right. As Arbeloa is in a deep position in which prevents him from providing support ahead of the new ball carrier, so Higuain moves to exploit the free space in behind No.3.

Higuain receives the pass from Di Maria. Khedira moves to provide support behind him and Kaka takes up a centre forward's position.

Kaka receives the diagonal pass in behind the opposition's defence and can either get a low cross into Ronaldo (option 1) or pass to the edge of the area for Khedira (option 2).

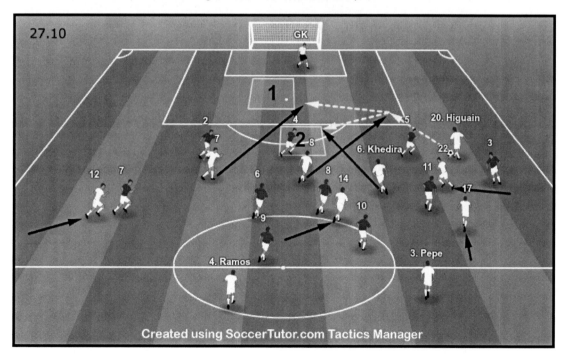

LONG DIAGONAL PASS TO THE CENTRE FORWARD

On diagram 27.11, Benzema makes a run between No.5 and No.3 to receive the long ball from Alonso.

 ## ASSESSMENT:

Real Madrid also used long passes sometimes to reach the opposition's penalty area more quickly and shoot on goal.

The forwards would mainly use the gap between the full back and the central defender on the weak side to make their runs into the penalty area from long balls.

EXAMPLE 2

On diagram 27.12, this time it is Di Maria who drops back, receives and plays a long ball towards Ronaldo.

 ## ASSESSMENT:

The full back (17. Arbeloa) and the winger (22. Di Maria) were very rarely both in wide positions on the right. The team was much more balanced on the right than the left.

BUILDING UP FROM THE BACK USING A LONG BALL

When Real Madrid were under pressure, their main aim was not to lose possession with a risky pass in a critical part of the field. The goalkeeper or the defenders preferred to hit a long ball towards the forwards rather than make a risky short pass to a midfielder who was under pressure.

When Casillas was the man in possession and the pressure was being applied from the right side, his long kick usually targeted Ronaldo. Ronaldo was very effective at winning aerial duels and Mourinho wanted to take advantage of this when the opposition were applying pressure.

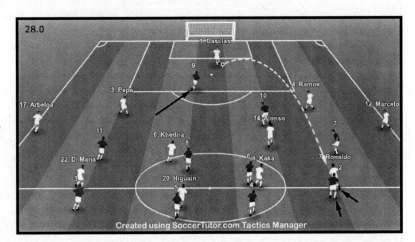

The attacking midfielder (option 1) would look to exploit the free space behind the opposition right back every time Ronaldo went to head a long ball.

On diagram 28.1, the centre forward (Higuain) also makes a move to receive behind the opposition's defensive line (option 2). The rest of the Real Madrid players (including Casillas) move towards the ball zone creating superiority in numbers. The centre forward (No.9) is left in an offside Position.

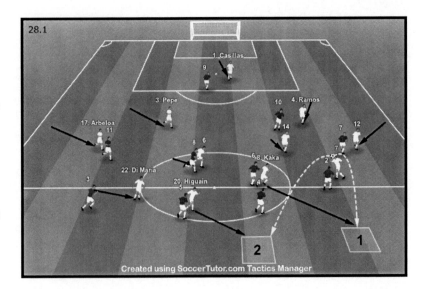

When Alonso dropped deep to take part in the team's build up play from the back and the attacking midfielder also moved a few yards back to retain the team's balance, the centre forward was the man who would take advantage of Ronaldo's header (diagrams 28.2, 28.3).

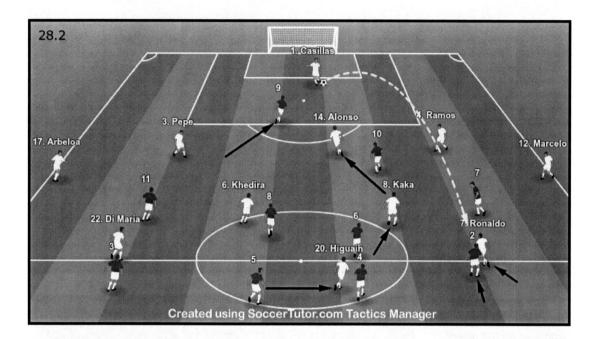

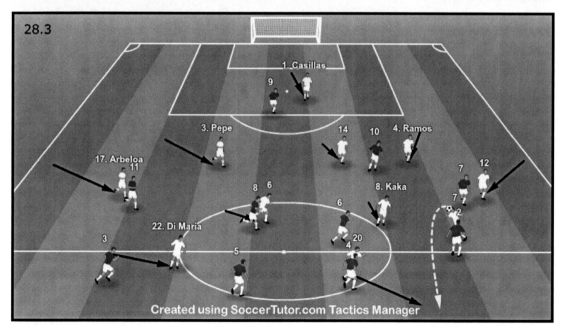

On diagram 28.4, the long pass is made by Pepe towards Higuain.

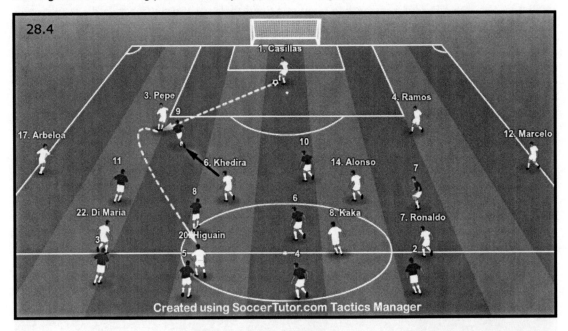

Di Maria moves to take advantage of a potential header while the rest of the players move towards the area the ball was directed.

 # ASSESSMENT:

When long balls towards the forwards were used, the team did not react passively. Mourinho's teams used long balls as a way of moving the ball quickly up the pitch and attempting to win possession near to the opposition's penalty area.

All the Real Madrid players moved forward quickly in synchronisation to outnumber the opposition around the ball zone and increase the possibility of winning the second ball.

CHAPTER 6

TRANSITIONS

TRANSITION FROM ATTACK TO DEFENCE

Under Mourinho's guidance, Real Madrid became very effective during both the negative and positive transitions.

During the negative transition, Madrid's main aim was to apply immediate pressure on the ball carrier as soon as possession was lost. For Real to be successful during this phase of play, the team had to remain compact, balanced and have a safety player in the appropriate position to apply pressure on the ball. The success of the team in this particular phase of play was key for them to dominate possession throughout their matches.

The safety player was usually in a supporting position behind the man in possession and would be available for a potential pass back or to apply immediate pressure on the ball if possession was lost.

Alonso was by far the most important player for Real Madrid during the negative transitions. Alonso had the role of the safety player in most of the team's negative transitions and could analyse tactical situations extremely quickly.

For Madrid's style of play to be effective, Alonso was the key. He would always take up the appropriate positions, reacting well to varying tactical situations raised on the field. His positional sense and defensive abilities often lead his team to regain possession immediately after losing it.

On diagram 29.0, the right back (Arbeloa) is in a position which enables him to react effectively to whatever Khedira decides to do. If Khedira manages to get past his direct opponent (No.8), Arbeloa can move forward to receive in the free space down the flank. If Khedira loses possession, Arbeloa is in a good position to contest the opposition's winger (No.11).

The diagrams to follow present 2 situations that show how the full backs took advantage of their good positioning to either move forward and receive or drop back to take up an effective defensive positions.

RETAINING POSSESSION

On diagrams 29.1 and 29.2 both full backs take up appropriate positions against the opposition's wingers. When Khedira manages to pass the ball to Ozil who is free of marking, Marcelo moves into an advanced position ready to receive.

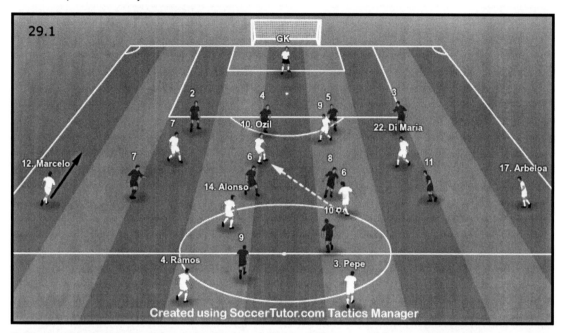

Ozil passes the ball to Marcelo on the flank and Alonso shifts to provide cover for Marcelo.

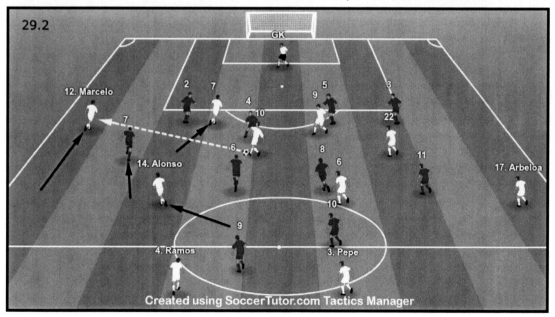

APPLYING IMMEDIATE PRESSURE WHEN POSSESSION IS LOST

On diagrams 29.3 and 29.4 the situation is different. Khedira's pass is intercepted by No.6.

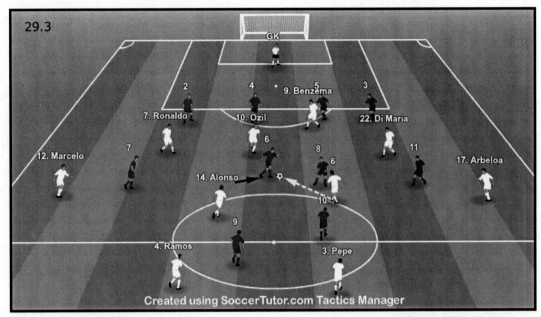

Marcelo and Arbeloa move towards the centre to take up goal side positions against the winger. Alonso and Khedira are the 2 safety players who move to block No.6's available passing options.

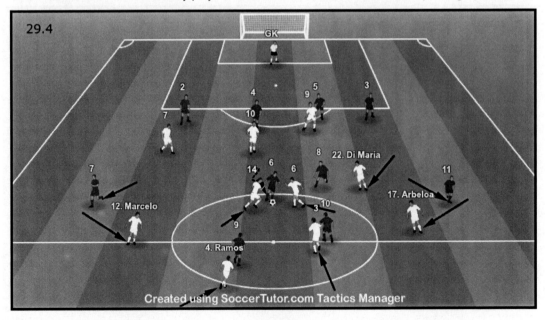

 # ASSESSMENT:

An important element of Real Madrid's negative and positive transition play was the full back's appropriate positioning against the opposing winger. The positioning of the full backs helped the team to retain its balance and be effective during the transitions.

When the ball was lost, the full backs would attempt to take up effective defensive positions against the opposing wingers immediately.

When the team regained possession, the full backs moved into advanced positions ready to receive a potential forward pass free of marking.

DEFENSIVE MIDFIELDER MAINTAINING BALANCE AND COHESION

On diagram 29.5, Ramos moves forward with the ball. Alonso drops back to provide cover. He is the safety player in this particular situation.

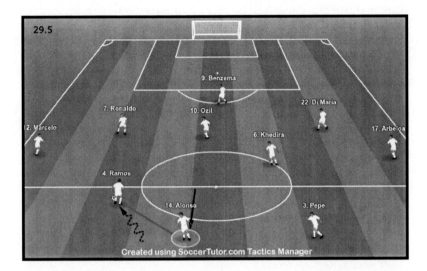

In a similar situation to the previous one, where the only difference is that it develops on the right. Pepe moves forward and Alonso drops back.

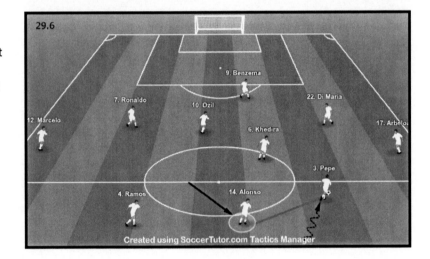

 # ASSESSMENT:

The holding midfielder dropped back into a central defender's position to retain the team's balance when the central defender moved forward with the ball.

THE NEGATIVE TRANSITION

During the negative transitions, Real Madrid had to deal mainly with 3 different situations.

1. Situations which favoured applying immediate pressure on the man in possession near the sidelines or in the centre.

2. Situations which did not favour applying immediate pressure on the man in possession near the sidelines or in the centre.

3. Situations which took place near the sidelines and where Real Madrid were outnumbered by the opposition.

When applying immediate pressure on the ball was possible:

During the first situation, Real's safety player could immediately put pressure on the ball carrier to restrict his available time and space. This was often because the opposition player who intercepted the ball did not have clear possession of the ball or because when he intercepted the ball he did not have time to search for available passing options (possibly he had his back turned to Madrid's goal). The rest of the Real players seek to mark all the opponents placed near the ball zone tightly. The central defender on the strong side marked his direct opponent closely, while the central defender on the weak side provided cover for him.

During the second situation, Real Madrid's safety player had to deal with an opponent who had enough time and space to search for the right pass after intercepting the ball. If this situation took place in the centre of the field, the safety player did not move to close him down, but tried to force the ball wide. If the possession was lost near the sideline, the safety player tried to prevent the man in possession from passing towards the centre and sought to keep the ball on one side to give time to the rest of the players to recover. The defenders tracked their direct opponents if they made runs in in behind the defensive line.

In the third situation, when the ball possession was lost near the sideline and the safety player was outnumbered, the safety player would not move forward to put pressure on the ball, but instead dropped back and left the defensive midfielder to take over the first defender role. The defensive midfielder would look to keep the ball on the same side to give his teammates time to recover and take up defensive positions. The defenders tracked their direct opponents if they made forward runs.

WINNING THE BALL BACK IN THE CENTRAL ZONE

On diagrams 29.7 and 29.8, the possession is lost in the centre of the field and the ball ends up with No.6 who receives with his back to Real Madrid's goal.

Alonso (the safety player) applies pressure without hesitation which prevents him from being able to turn and search for available passing options. The rest of the players move to mark all the other players near the ball zone tightly. Pepe provides cover for Ramos.

CHAPTER 6

WHEN IMMEDIATE REGAINING OF POSSESSION IS NOT POSSIBLE

On diagrams 29.9 and
29.10, No.2 wins the ball
and moves forward.

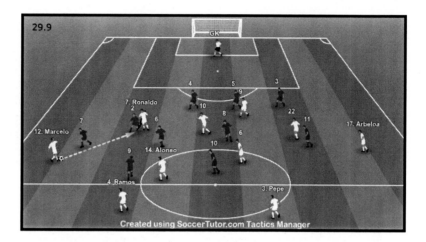

As the new man in possession has enough time on the ball to search for the right pass, the
opposition's players (No.7, No.9 and No.10) move to receive a pass towards the free space.

Ramos follows No.9's run,
Marcelo moves towards
the centre to retain a goal
side position against No.7
and Pepe drops back to
provide cover for Ramos.
At the same time, Pepe
keeps an eye on No.10.
Arbeloa recovers to create
superiority in numbers.
The safety player (Alonso)
takes up a position
which enables him to
prevent a pass towards
the centre, as does Ozil.
With this reaction time is
gained for the rest of the
players (Khedira, Di Maria,
Arbeloa) to recover.

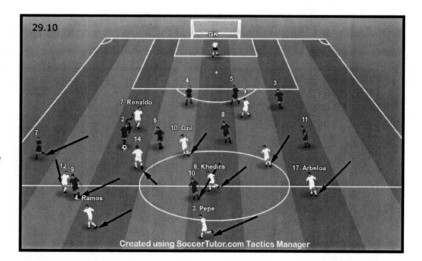

PREVENTING THE SWITCH OF PLAY

On diagrams 29.11 and 29.12, the possession is lost on the left and the opposition outnumber Marcelo (No.2 & No.7).

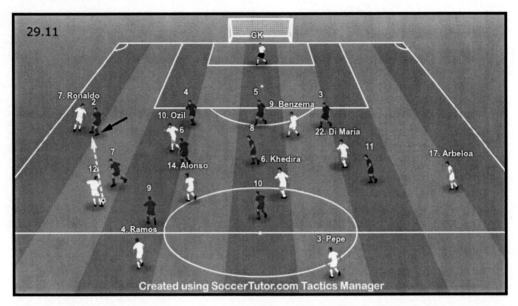

Marcelo is the safety player so does not move forward to contest the man in possession, but follows No.7's movement instead and leaves Alonso to take over the role of the first defender. Alonso and Ozil try to keep the ball on the left and give time to the rest of the players to recover into effective defensive positions. Ramos follows No.9's run collaboration with Pepe and Arbeloa tucks in to provide superiority in numbers.

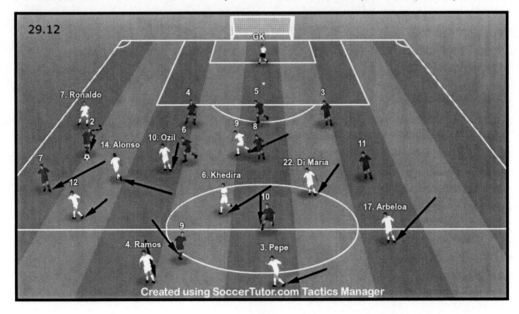

SAFETY PLAYERS

The next diagrams show how Real Madrid retained their balance and which player took the role of safety player during the team's attacking moves. There are also diagrams which present how other similar situations progressed during matches.

On diagram 29.13, Marcelo is the man in possession and is placed near to the sideline. Alonso and Ramos move and take up positions which provide safety in case possession is lost.

TEAM COHESION: REGAINING POSSESSION

On diagrams 29.14 and 29.15, we show how the diagram 29.13 situation progresses during games. Marcelo's attempt to get past his direct opponent on the left is unsuccessful.

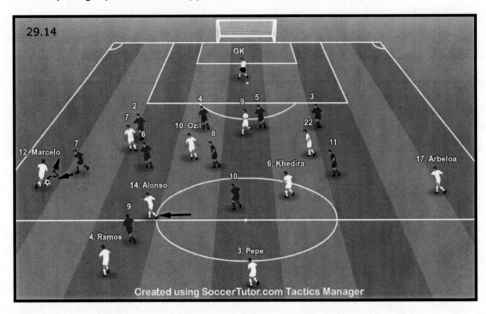

No.7 wins the ball and moves forward. Alonso (the safety player) moves to close him down while Ramos shifts across to mark No.9. Pepe provides cover for him and Khedira shifts towards the centre to provide balance in midfield. Arbeloa tucks in to be the third defender at the back.

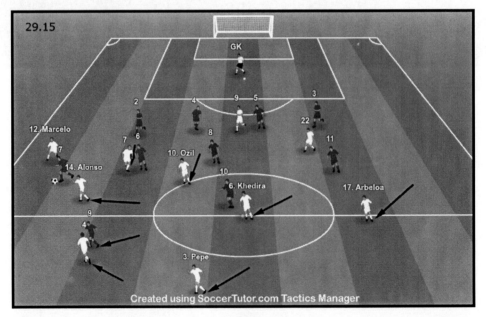

SAFETY PLAYERS: THE LEFT SIDE

On diagram 29.16 Ronaldo is the man in possession and he is placed towards the centre. Both Marcelo and Alonso are the safety players and are positioned in covering positions.

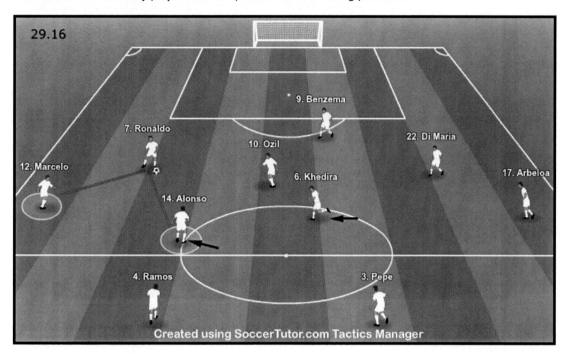

 # ASSESSMENT:

Retaining the team's balance on the left came from the good collaboration between Marcelo and Alonso because Ronaldo had a free role. So the left back and the holding midfielder had to take up positions in relation to Ronaldo's positioning so they would not leave the team unbalanced.

When Ronaldo was in an advanced position, Marcelo stayed deep to provide cover. When both of them moved forward, Alonso shifted towards the left to provide safety and keep the team balanced.

REGAINING POSSESSION IN THE CENTRE OF THE FIELD

On diagrams 29.17 and 29.18, the pass is directed to Ronaldo. No.6 of the opposition contests him and wins the ball.

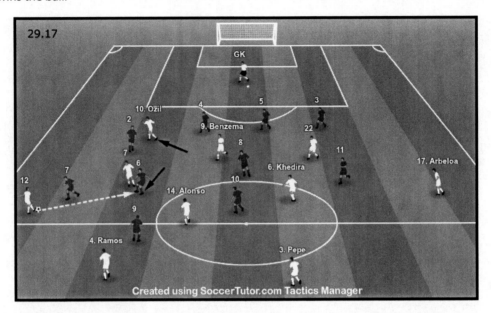

As No.6 has not got clear possession of the ball, Alonso reacts immediately and puts pressure on him. Ramos tightens No.9's marking and Pepe provides cover. Marcelo and Arbeloa move towards the centre taking up effective defensive positions, while Khedira shifts to provide balance and mark No.10 who is near the ball zone.

SAFETY PLAYERS: RONALDO'S DRIVING RUNS

On diagram 29.19, both Marcelo and Ronaldo move into advanced positions. Alonso makes an extensive shift towards the left side to provide cover and takes over the left back's role. Khedira does the same thing and takes up a central position to provide balance in midfield. Alonso and Khedira are the safety players.

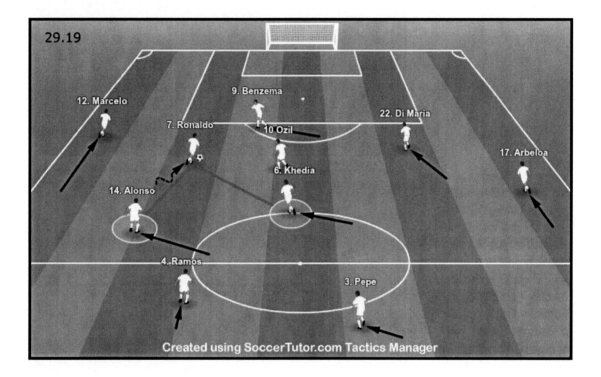

LIMITING PASSING OPTIONS FOR THE NEW BALL CARRIER

On diagrams 29.20 up to 29.22, Ronaldo loses possession. No.6 wins the ball and tries to move forward.

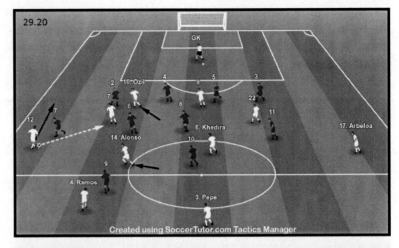

Alonso and Khedira apply immediate pressure so they can block all the available options for the new ball carrier. In case Alonso is unable to win the ball back immediately, Khedira must make sure that the ball is not passed towards the centre, so he moves to block off the passing lane towards No.10.

Arbeloa is then able to recover and take up an effective position and ensure superiority in numbers.

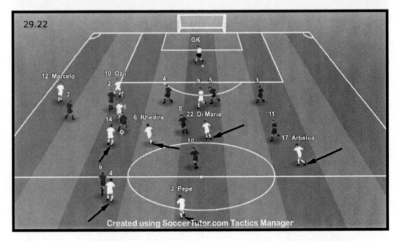

SAFETY PLAYERS: FULL BACK'S INSIDE MOVEMENT

On diagram 29.23, Ronaldo has possession down the flank. Marcelo moves towards the centre to provide cover in case the ball is lost. Alonso is able to move higher up the field because of Marcelo's position.

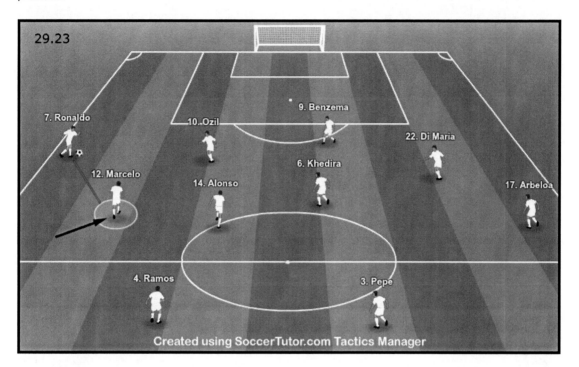

WINNING THE BALL BACK IN AN ADVANCED WIDE POSITION

On diagrams 29.24 up to 29.26, Marcelo passes the ball to Ronaldo who is placed near the sideline and takes up a supporting position behind him.

No.2 and No.7 of the opposition challenge Ronaldo and win the ball.

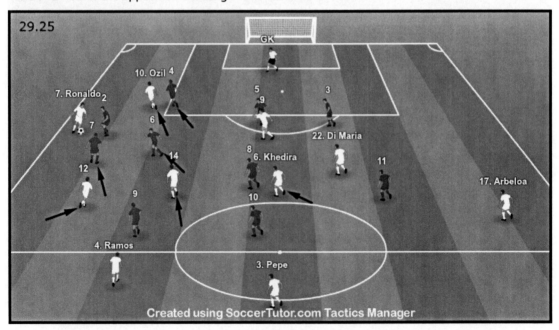

Marcelo immediately puts pressure on the new ball carrier and Alonso makes sure that the ball remains on the left by taking up a position towards the inside of the field. Ramos marks No.9 and Pepe shifts to provide cover. Khedira provides balance in midfield and Arbeloa moves towards the centre.

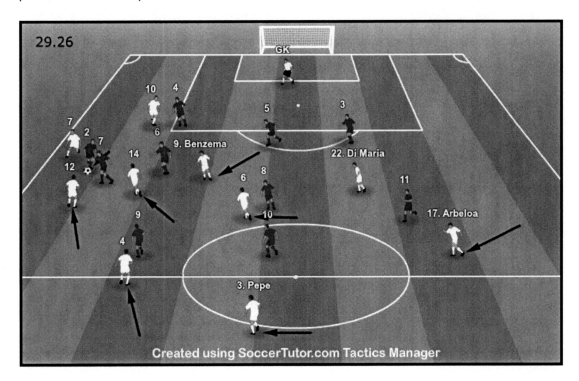

 ## ASSESSMENT:

In situations where the possession was lost in the centre and the Real Madrid players could not ensure the immediate regaining of possession, the midfielders made sure that the ball was forced out wide. This action gained time for the rest of the players to recover into effective defensive positions.

SAFETY PLAYERS: ALONSO'S COVERING ON THE LEFT SIDE

On diagram 29.27, Alonso moves into Marcelo's position who makes an inside run.

KEEPING THE OPPOSITION NEAR THE SIDELINE

On diagrams 29.28 and 29.29, Marcelo passes the ball to Ronaldo and makes an inside run. Alonso assesses the tactical situation and shifts towards the left to provide cover.

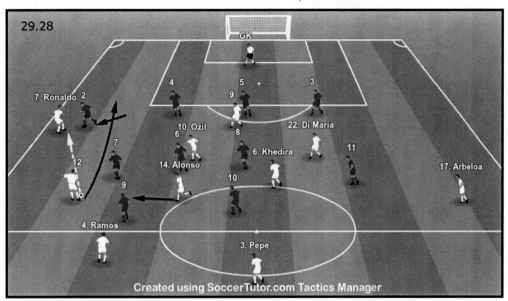

When Ronaldo loses possession to No.2, Alonso is close enough to apply immediate pressure. He seeks to keep the ball on the left in case the immediate regaining of possession is not possible. Ozil also shifts to provide support and Ramos follows No.9's movement towards the sideline. Pepe provides cover and Khedira makes an extensive shift towards the left to provide balance.

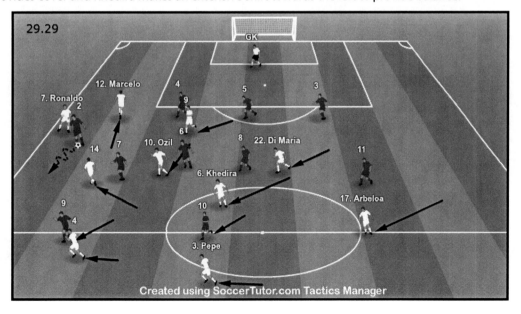

SAFETY PLAYERS: IN THE CENTRE OF THE FIELD

On diagram 29.30, the ball is with Ozil. Alonso and Khedira are the safety players.

On diagram 29.31, Ronaldo is on the flank and about to put a cross into the box. Marcelo moves into a covering position as the safety player. Alonso is able to move further up the pitch because of Marcelo's positioning.

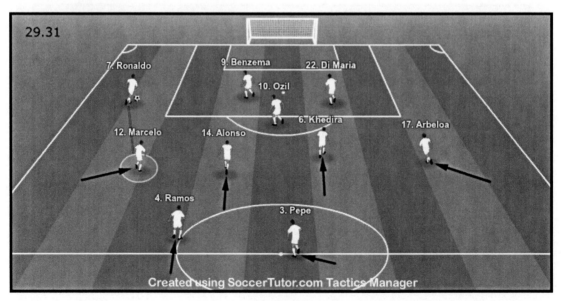

LOSING POSSESSION NEAR THE OPPOSITION PENALTY AREA

On diagrams 29.32 up to 29.34, the ball has moved from the right to left. Ronaldo loses possession to No.2 on the flank.

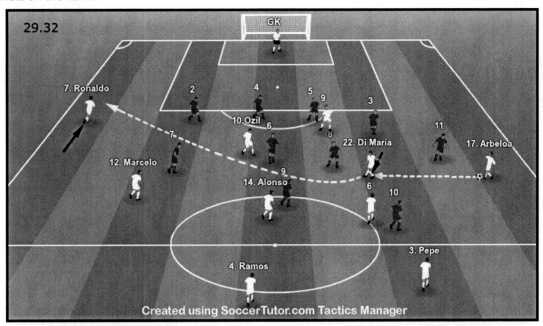

Marcelo (the safety player) applies pressure on the new man in possession and Alonso tracks No.7's run.

Benzema and Ozil shift towards the left to block a possible pass towards the centre. Khedira moves to provide balance after Alonso's extensive shift. Ramos has no player to mark so moves towards the strong side to deal with a potential long pass from No.2. Arbeloa moves back and creates superiority in numbers for Real.

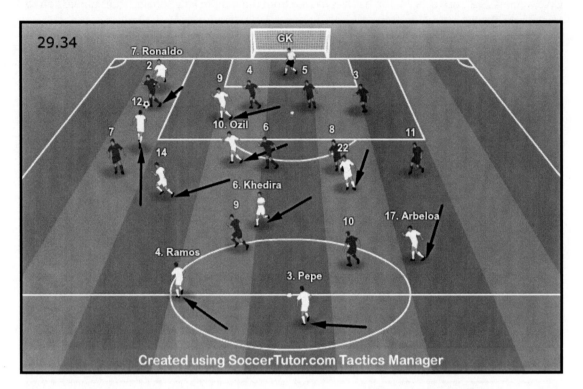

Created using SoccerTutor.com Tactics Manager

 ## ASSESSMENT:

When possession was lost near to the sideline, the Real Madrid player who took over the role of the first defender sought to regain the ball immediately.

If the immediate regaining of possession was not possible, the main aim would be to keep the ball near the sideline to allow time for the rest of the players to recover and take up effective defensive positions.

SAFETY PLAYERS: ADVANCED SUPPORTING POSITIONS

On diagram 29.35, Marcelo is the player who gets ready to make a cross into the opposition's penalty area. Alonso moves towards the left and he and Ozil are the two safety players.

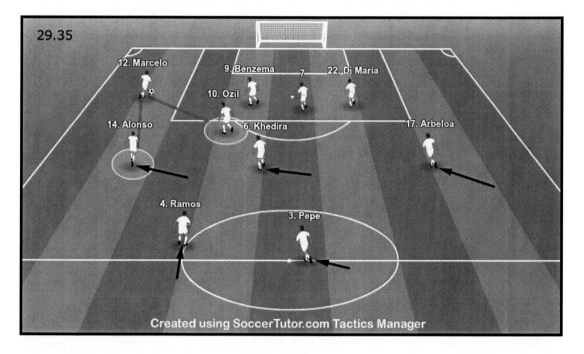

LOSING POSSESSION NEAR THE OPPOSITION PENALTY AREA (2)

On diagrams 29.36 up to 29.38, Madrid switch the play from right to left. Marcelo moves down the flank but loses possession to No.2, who then makes a pass to No.7.

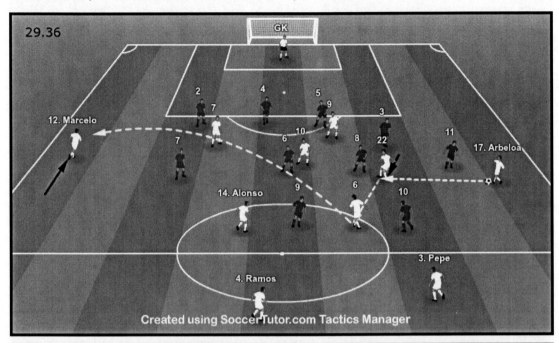

Alonso applies pressure immediately and together with Ozil (the second safety player) double marks the new man in possession. Khedira marks No.9 and there is already a superiority in numbers in defence.

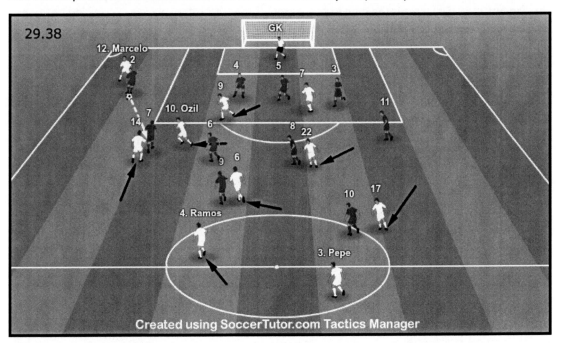

SAFETY PLAYERS: SUPPORTING THE FORWARD

On diagram 29.39, Benzema is the man in possession. There are 3 safety players in covering positions who are ready to react to a possible loss of possession.

COHESION: CLOSING DOWN IN NUMBERS

On diagrams 29.40 and 29.41, the pass is made towards Benzema, but No.4 intercepts the ball.

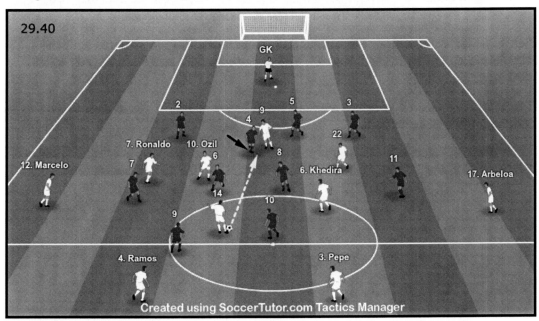

Ozil and Di Maria move to double mark the new ball carrier while Alonso and Khedira block the pass to No.10 and No.8 respectively. Pepe and Ramos move forward to reduce the distance to their direct opponents in case there is a pass directed to them. The full backs shift inwards to take

 # ASSESSMENT:

The retaining of balance on the right side during negative transitions resulted from the good collaboration between the full back, the winger and the defensive midfielder.

When the winger dropped deep, the full back could move forward into an advanced position as there was already a safety player (this usually took place on the right as Di Maria was very reliable defensively).

When both of them were in advanced positions, the defensive midfielder shifted towards the sideline to take up the role of the full back.

In cases where all 3 players (Di Maria, Arbeloa and Khedira) on the right were in advanced positions, the holding midfielder (Alonso) made an extensive shift towards the right to provide cover.

SAFETY PLAYERS: THE RIGHT SIDE

On diagram 29.42, Di Maria has possession. Arbeloa and Khedira are the 2 safety players.

On diagrams 29.43 and 29.44, No.3 of the opposition intercepts the pass from Arbeloa. Khedira moves to close him down immediately. Arbeloa moves to double mark while Ozil moves to mark No.8. Pepe moves forward and marks No.10 tightly. Ramos shifts towards the right to provide cover. Alonso moves also towards the strong side.

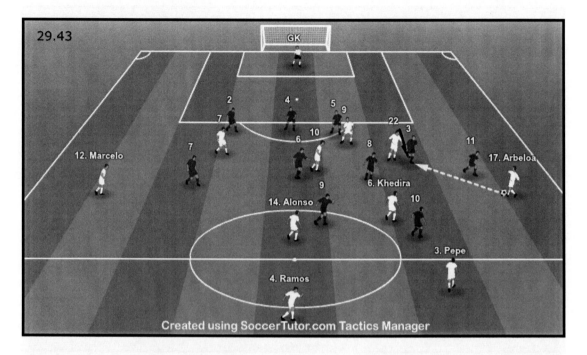

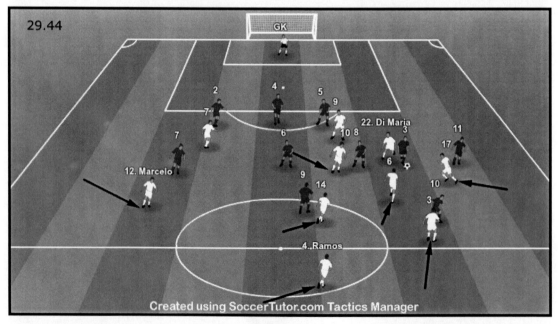

SAFETY PLAYERS: INSIDE RIGHT POSITIONS

On diagram 29.45, Arbeloa moves into an advanced position. Khedira shifts towards the right, as does Alonso. These 2 are the safety players in this tactical context.

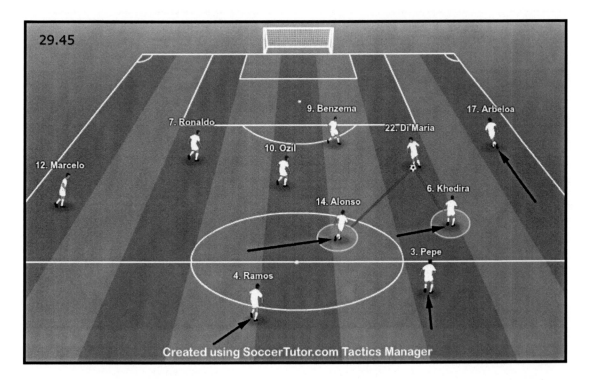

CREATING A 5 v 2 NUMERICAL ADVANTAGE AROUND THE BALL ZONE

On diagrams 29.46 up to 29.48, No.11 wins the 1v1 against Di Maria and moves forward with the ball.

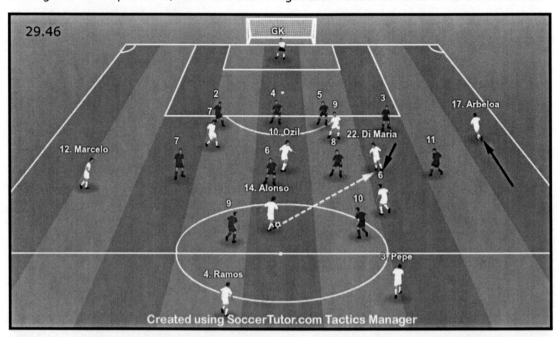

Both Alonso and Khedira move to double mark No.11, while Ozil blocks a potential pass towards the centre. Pepe moves forward and marks No.10 tightly and Ramos provides cover. Marcelo recovers to be the third man in defence.

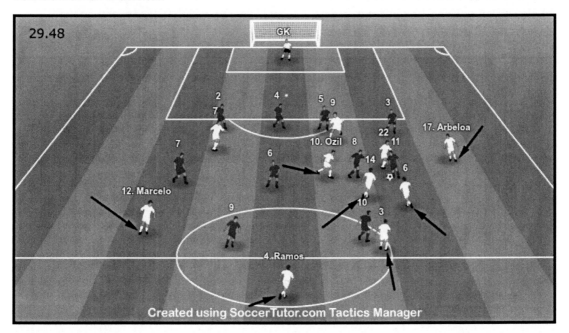

SAFETY PLAYERS: THE RIGHT FLANK

On diagram 29.49, Di Maria has possession near to the sideline. Khedira makes an inside run and Arbeloa moves towards the centre into a defensive midfielder's position to take over the safety player's role. Alonso shifts towards the strong side.

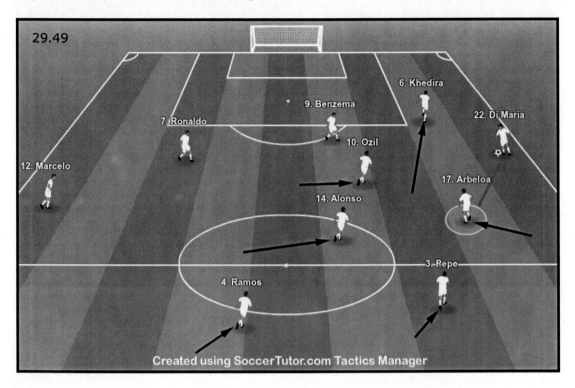

TRACKING RUNNERS ON A COUNTER ATTACK

On diagrams 29.50 up to 29.52, there is a long ball from Ramos to Di Maria on the right flank. He is under No.3's pressure and loses possession.

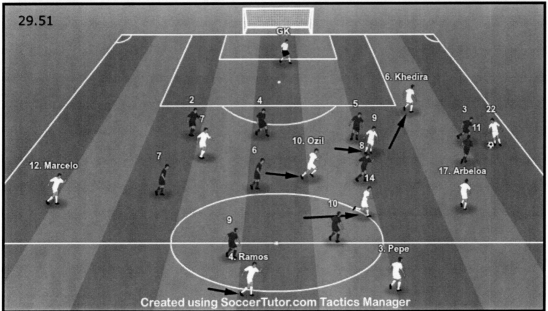

As No.11 makes a run towards the side there is a 2v1 situation, Arbeloa does not move to challenge the ball carrier, but follows No.11's run instead.

Alonso moves to close No.3 down and keep the ball on the right. Benzema shifts across to block a potential pass towards No.8 and Ozil drops back to provide balance. Pepe marks No.10, Ramos provides cover as well as keeping an eye on No.9. Marcelo shifts back to create superiority in numbers.

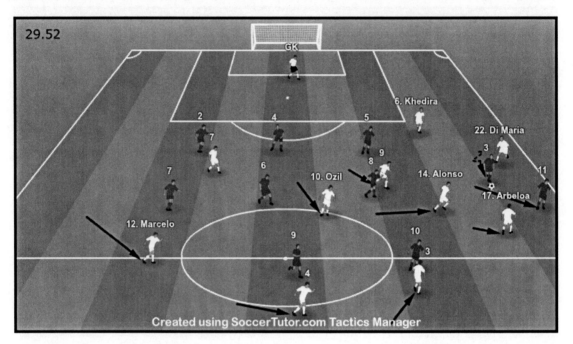

SAFETY PLAYERS: THE RIGHT FLANK (2)

On diagram 29.53, Arbeloa makes an inside run and Khedira shifts towards the right to provide safety in case possession is lost.

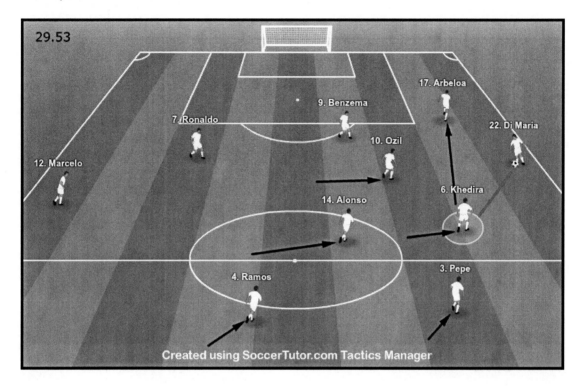

TRACKING RUNNERS ON A COUNTER ATTACK (2)

On diagrams 29.54 up to 29.56, the pass is directed to Di Maria on the right. Arbeloa makes an inside run and Khedira shifts across to provide cover for him.

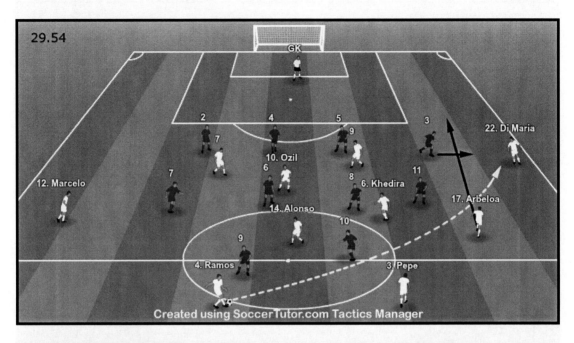

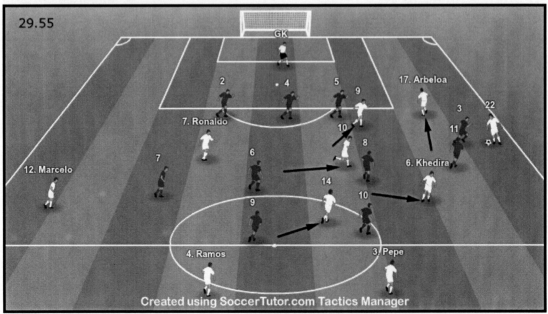

As No.3 wins the ball and moves forward, Khedira shifts across to close him down immediately. Alonso also makes an extensive shift to provide balance and together with Ozil makes sure that the ball remains on the right. Pepe follows No.10 and Ramos provides cover.

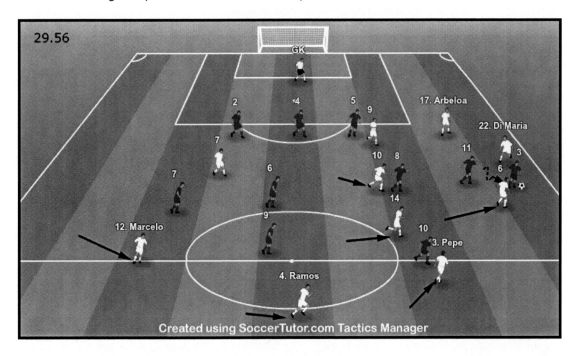

SAFETY PLAYERS: ALONSO'S COVERING POSITION

On diagram 29.57, both Arbeloa and Khedira take up advanced positions. That is why Alonso is forced to make an extensive shift towards the right side to provide safety.

ENSURING SUPERIORITY IN NUMBERS AT THE BACK

On diagrams 29.58 up to 29.60, after receiving a long ball from Ramos, Di Maria loses possession to No.3. Alonso had made an extensive shift towards the right so he is the one who moves to apply pressure on the ball carrier. The aim again is to keep the ball on the same side if the immediate regaining of possession is not possible.

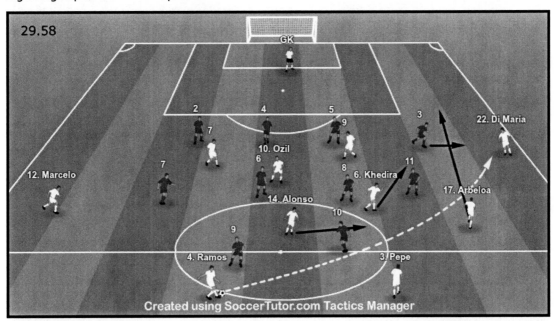

Khedira also moves towards the ball carrier to block a potential pass into the centre, while Ozil drops back to provide balance in midfield. Pepe and Ramos keep an eye on No.10 and No.9 respectively as they shift towards the strong side. Marcelo moves to create superiority in numbers at the back.

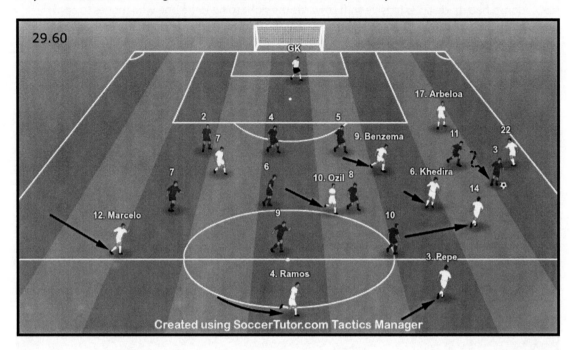

SAFETY PLAYERS: KHEDIRA'S ADVANCED POSITION

On diagram 29.61, Arbeloa is in a position which provides safety if possession is lost. Khedira has the opportunity to move into a more advanced position as Arbeloa is already placed in the appropriate position.

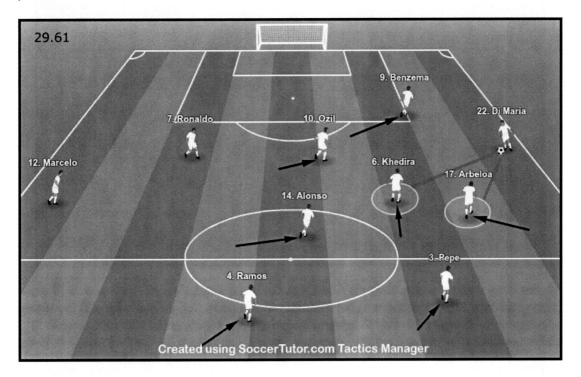

SHIFTING ACROSS INTO COVERING POSITIONS

On diagrams 29.62 and 29.63, Di Maria loses possession to No.3.

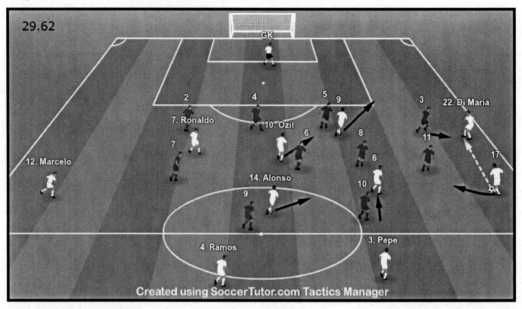

Arbeloa immediately moves to close the new ball carrier down. Khedira assists him in keeping the ball on the right as he moves to prevent a potential pass towards No.11. Ozil shifts also towards the strong side marking No.8. Pepe marks No.10 closely as he makes a move towards the sideline to receive. Ramos provides cover for Pepe and Marcelo moves towards the centre to be the third man in defence.

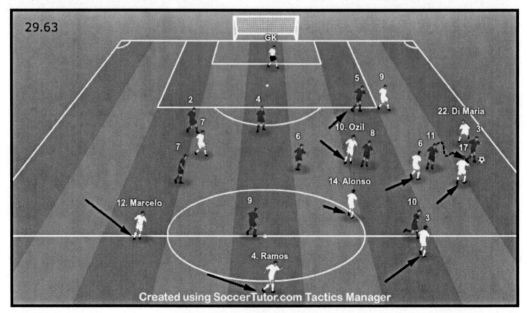

SAFETY PLAYERS: SUPPORT PLAY NEAR THE PENALTY AREA

On diagram 29.64, Di Maria is on the right flank and is ready to cross into the penalty area. Arbeloa and Khedira provide safety.

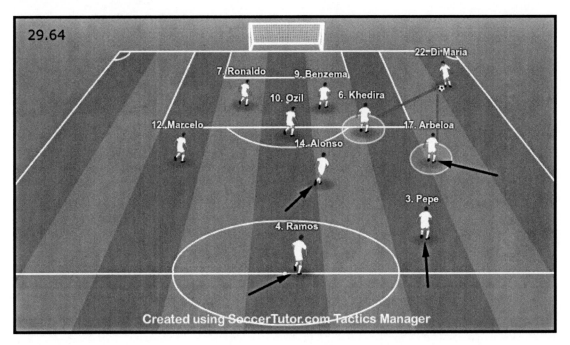

SUPERIORITY IN NUMBERS HIGH UP THE PITCH

On diagrams 29.65 up to 29.67, Di Maria makes an inside run, receives the pass on the right flank and gets a cross into the box. No.5 clears the ball and it is directed to No.11.

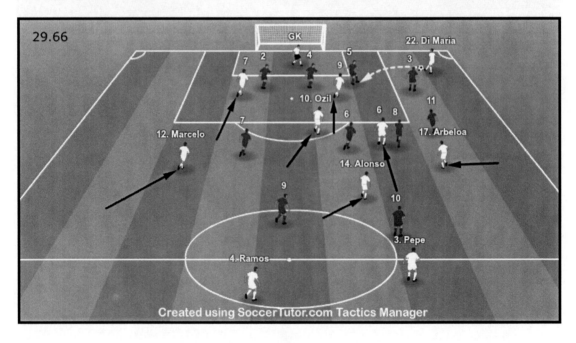

Arbeloa and Khedira apply pressure immediately on No.11. Ozil moves to block a potential pass towards the centre. Alonso and Pepe mark No.10, while Ramos and Marcelo provide superiority in numbers.

SAFETY PLAYERS: NEAR TO THE BYLINE

On diagram 29.68, Arbeloa has possession in an advanced position on the flank and is ready to cross the ball.

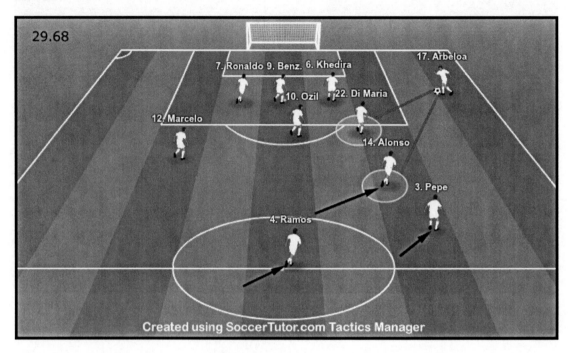

As Khedira takes up a position in the penalty area, Di Maria has to provide safety. Alonso sees Khedira's position and makes an extensive shift towards the right and takes the role of the second safety player.

POSITIONING FOR CLEARANCES FROM CROSSES

On diagrams 29.69 up to 29.71, Arbeloa receives and gets a cross into the box. No.5 again clears the ball and it is directed to No.11.

Di Maria and Ozil apply immediate pressure on the ball carrier. Benzema moves to triple mark the new man in possession. Alonso marks No.10, while Pepe moves to clock a potential pass towards the sideline. Marcelo and Ramos keep an eye on No.9.

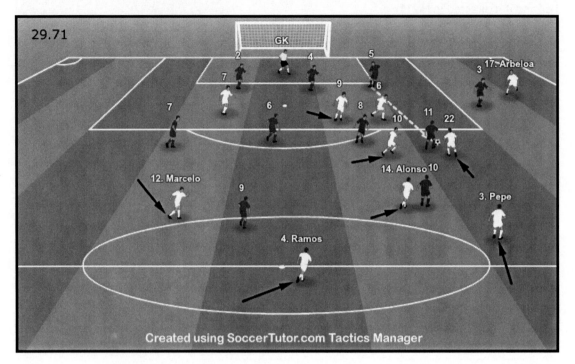

TRANSITION FROM DEFENCE TO ATTACK

During the positive transition, Real Madrid were said to be the most successful team in the world. Having players like Ronaldo Benzema, Di Maria and Ozil who could exploit the free spaces and make quality passes meant Mourinho prepared a team which could counter attack very effectively.

When Madrid won the ball in the midfield and the opposition blocked off all the available vertical and diagonal passing lanes, the team mainly sought to move the ball towards the weak side of the opposing team in order to exploit the potential free spaces. If there were not any available spaces, the team tried to retain possession.

When a vertical or a diagonal pass was possible, the team could very easily reach the opposition's penalty area and create chances.

When Real defended deep close to their own penalty area, Ronaldo's poor defensive positioning high up the pitch gave the team a great advantage. Ronaldo's positioning usually led to a 3v3 situation and plenty of available space to be exploited.

SWITCHING PLAY FROM THE STRONG SIDE TO THE WEAK SIDE

On diagrams 30.0 up to 30.2, Alonso wins the ball in midfield after Marcelo's intervention on the left. As there are no available passing lines for vertical and diagonal passes to be made, the team uses square passes to move the ball towards the weak side of the opposition.

Arbeloa's aggressive marking against No.11 during the defensive phase gives him the opportunity to move quickly into an advanced position and he is ready to take part in the attacking phase.

However, because of the opposition players' shift towards the right which restricts the available space, Real simply seek to retain possession. That is why Di Maria drops back to support Arbeloa and receive the pass.

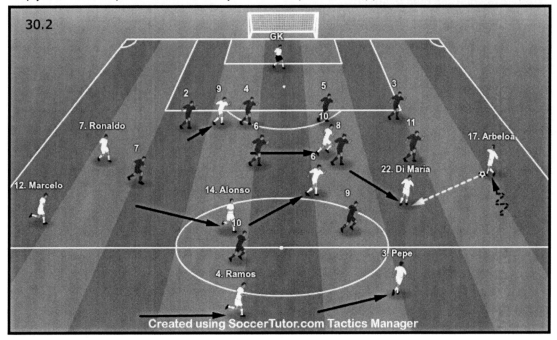

TRANSITION TO THE FINAL ATTACKING STAGE

On diagrams 30.3 up to 30.5, Alonso wins the ball in midfield again.

As the opposing players react quickly and block the potential vertical and diagonal passes, the ball is passed to Khedira and then to Arbeloa.

The right back (Arbeloa) has plenty of free space this time and takes advantage by moving forward. Di Maria makes an inside run towards the sideline to outnumber No.3 together with Arbeloa and receives. Benzema and Ozil move into the penalty area and Ronaldo moves to the edge of it to receive the cross from Di Maria.

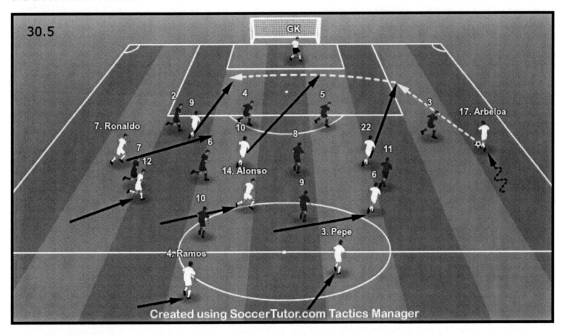

EXAMPLE 2

On diagrams 30.6 up to 30.8, Alonso intercepts the vertical pass and is put under pressure so passes to Khedira.

No.11 does not react quickly to block off the pass to Di Maria, so the Real winger is able to receive the diagonal pass and moves towards the opposition's penalty area.

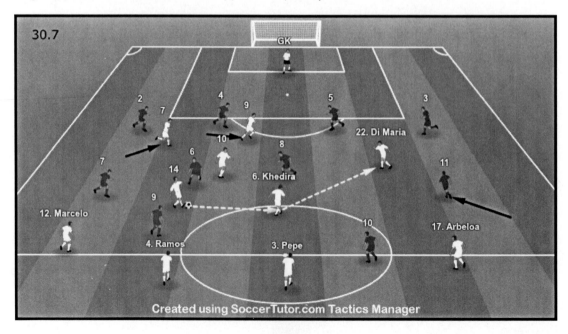

Benzema (option 1) and Ronaldo (option 2) move diagonally and are ready to receive a potential diagonal or vertical pass respectively. The man in possession also has the opportunity to shoot at goal (option 3).

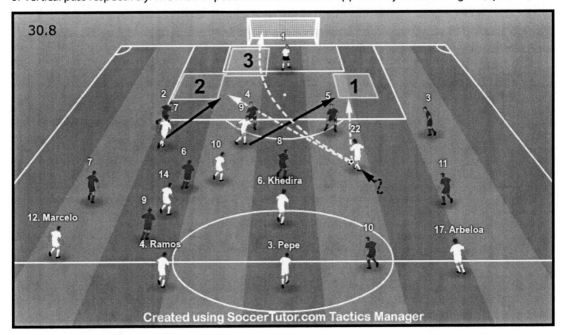

APPLYING IMMEDIATE PRESSURE ON THE BALL CARRIER

On diagrams 30.9 up to 30.11, the opposition's right back (No.2) moves into an advanced position. Ronaldo takes up a balanced position between him and the central defender. As the pass reaches No.7, Marcelo and Alonso apply double marking.

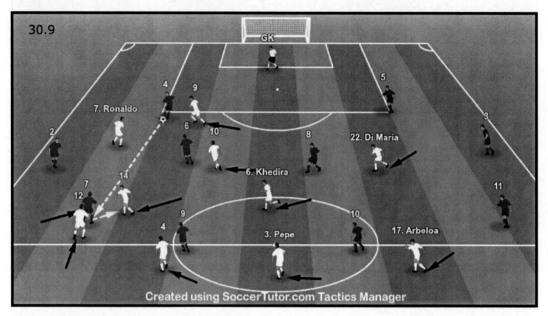

Alonso regains possession and immediately passes to Ronaldo before No.2 is able to take up a defensive position.

Ronaldo moves towards the centre while Benzema makes a diagonal move in behind No.4. Ozil moves to exploit the space created by Benzema. Ronaldo can make a pass to Ozil (option 1), to Benzema (option 2) or even shoot at goal (option 3).

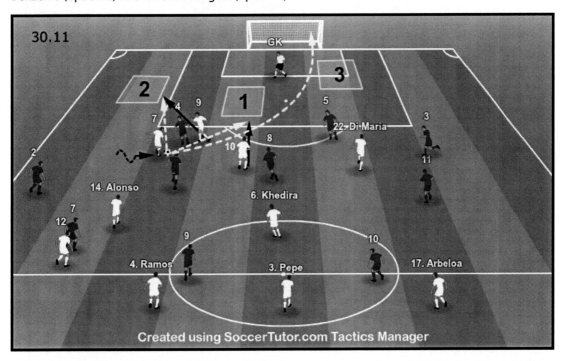

PRESSING NEAR THE SIDELINE: QUICK COUNTER ATTACK

On diagrams 30.12 up to 30.14, Ozil wins the ball in midfield this time.

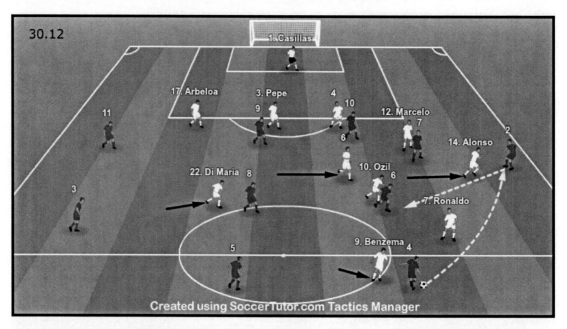

Ronaldo moves to a wide position and receives from Ozil.

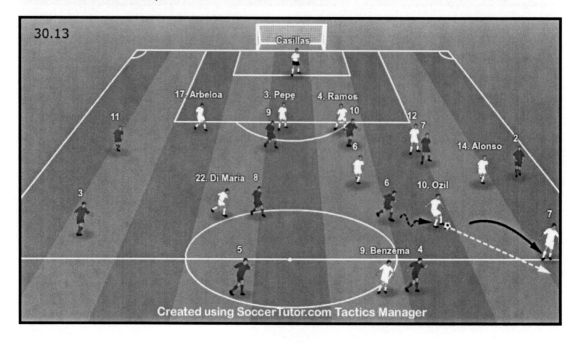

Benzema makes a run in behind No.4 and receives the ball and Ozil moves into the centre forward position. Ozil shoots on goal from Benzema's cross.

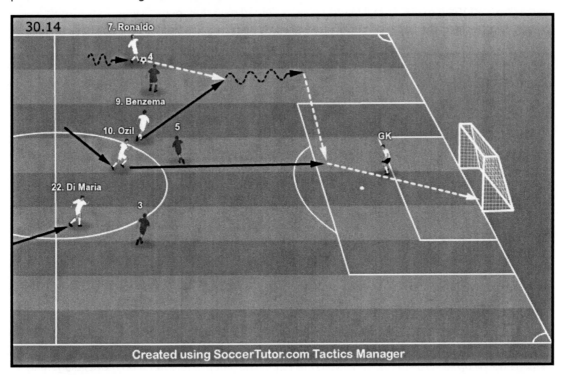

 # ASSESSMENT:

In a similar situation to the previous ones here, when Ronaldo received the ball near the sideline with plenty of free space to exploit in front of him, he would look to use his great ability in 1v1 situations on the flank.

COUNTER ATTACK FROM A DEFENSIVE CLEARANCE

On diagrams 30.15 up to 30.17, Real Madrid players defend near their penalty area. As No.7 gets a cross in, Ramos clears the ball and it is directed towards Benzema, who passes the ball back to Ozil.

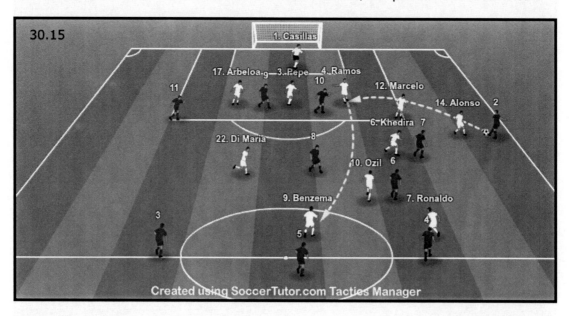

Di Maria opens up towards the sideline which stretches the defence and Ronaldo moves diagonally towards the centre.

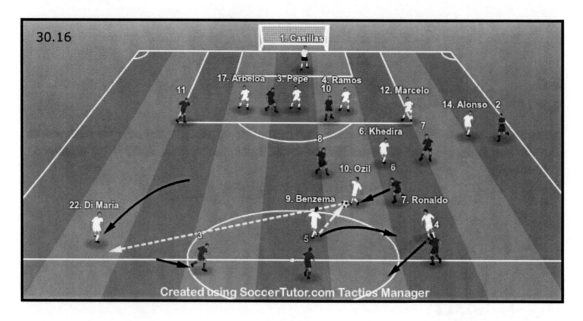

Ozil passes to Di Maria who moves forward with the ball and makes the final pass to Ronaldo who makes a diagonal run towards the free space.

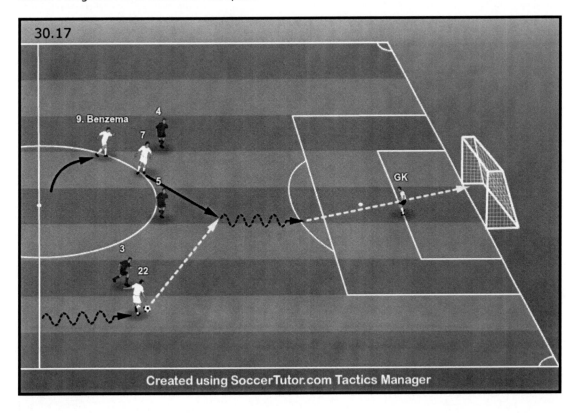

EXAMPLE 2

On diagrams 30.18 and 30.19, Khedira has possession after Pepe's header and moves forward with the ball and passes to Di Maria who makes a move towards the sideline

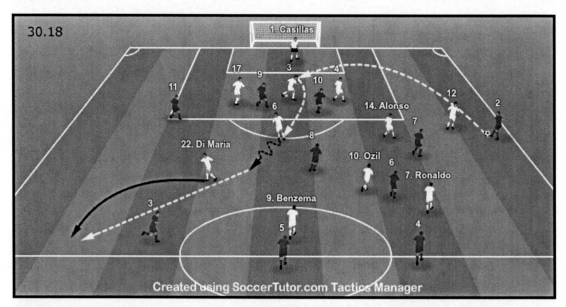

Benzema moves diagonally, receives the pass from Di Maria and crosses for Ronaldo.

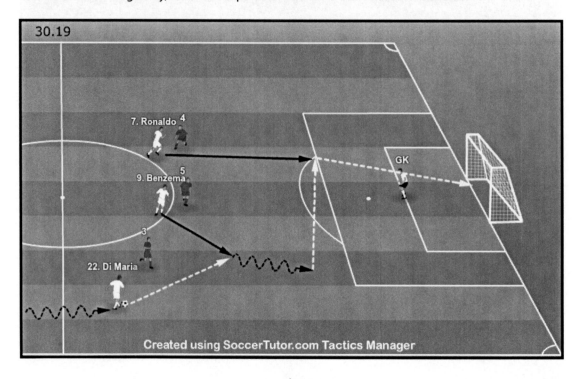

CHAPTER 7

REAL MADRID'S ATTACKING FROM SET PIECES

REAL MADRID'S ATTACKING SET PIECES

Most Real Madrid players were physically strong and tall. This made the side very effective when attacking from set pieces.

CORNER KICKS

During the corner kicks, 5 Real players took up positions inside the area. All the players (except for Khedira who was placed in the 6 yard box and near the goalkeeper) moved towards the opposition's goal to score with a header. Ronaldo, Pepe, Ramos and Benzema relied on their jumping height and physical strength to win aerial duels during corner kicks.

Mourinho placed 2 players outside the area to win any potential clearances. He also always kept a spare man at the back.

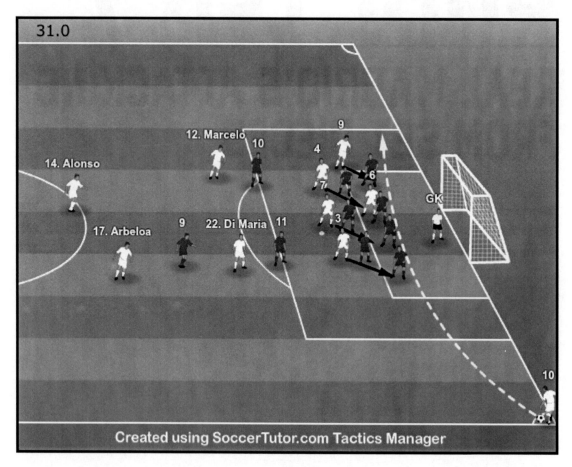

FREE KICKS NEAR THE SIDELINE

During free kicks near the corner flag, the team used a combination of movements in order for Ramos to get free of marking. Pepe, Ronaldo and Benzema would move towards the opposition's goal dragging their direct opponents out of positions to create space for him.

Ramos used to make a curved run into the free space which was usually between the penalty spot and the 6 yard box. There are also 2 players outside the penalty area (Marcelo and Di Maria) while Arbeloa had a deeper position ready to defend a potential long ball from the opposition.

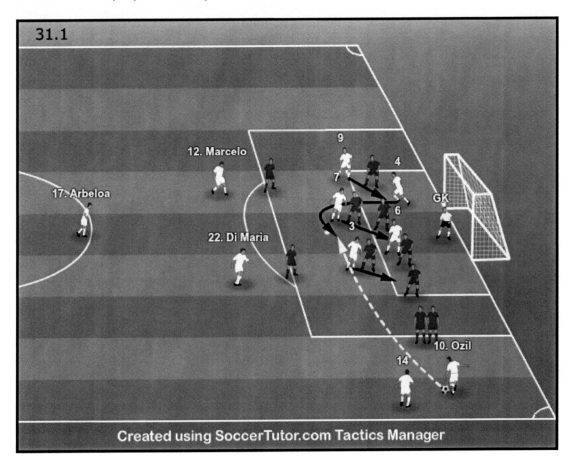

EXAMPLE 2

During free kicks in wide areas, there was usually an in swinging cross from Ozil on the right and Alonso on the left.

In this situation, 4 Real Madrid players (Benzema, Ronaldo, Ramos and Pepe) made a move towards the opposition's goal attempting to win a header. 2 players were placed just outside the area (Khedira and Di Maria) and 2 players were in deeper positions (Arbeloa and Marcelo).

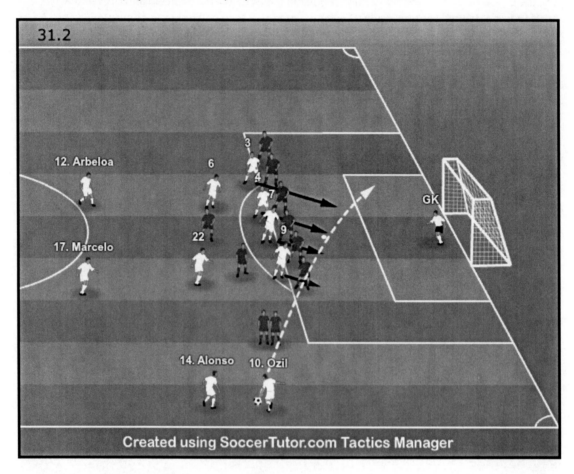

PLAYING WITH 10 MEN

When Real Madrid had a player sent off, Mourinho changed the formation to 4-4-1. When playing with 10 men, the team defended the zone passively near to the halfway line.

Ronaldo would try to retain a goal side defensive position against the opposition's right back and tracked him whenever he made forward runs. Ronaldo's positioning enabled Alonso to help the 2 central defenders and kept the team balanced.

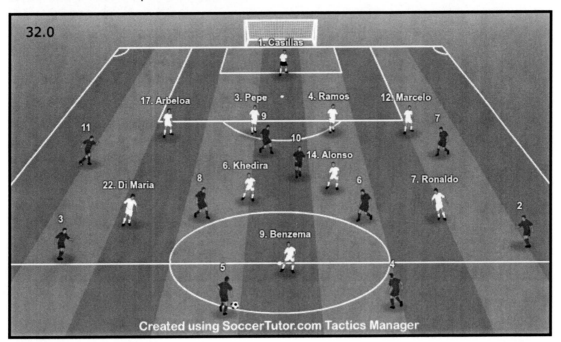

 ## ASSESSMENT:

When the opposition were putting crosses into the box, Alonso sought to take up a position inside the penalty area so Real would not to be outnumbered by the opposition.

Although there were changes when playing against 10 men, there were times when Real used their typical pressing in the 4-4-1 formation. Benzema's effort to create a strong side by forcing the opposition's build up play towards the side (diagram 32.1) was necessary for the effectiveness of this tactical reaction.

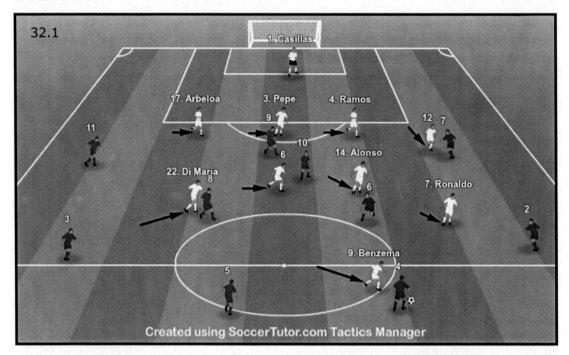

As Ronaldo had an effective goal side position against the right back, Alonso could focus on marking the midfielder (No.6) and Di Maria made an extensive shift towards the centre in order to provide support for Khedira. This would however, leave the opposition's No.3 completely

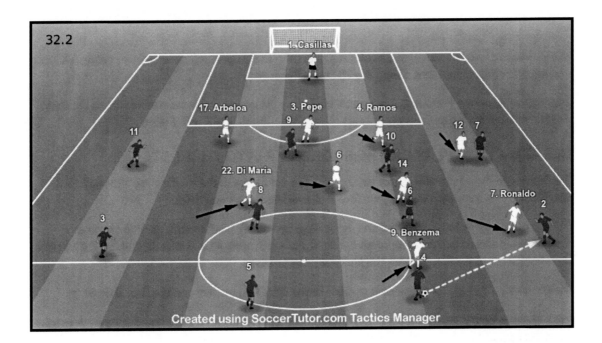

ASSESSMENT:

When Real Madrid had 10 men, they didn't risk building up from the back. They only attempted to build up play after regaining possession (in a positive transition).

CONCLUSION

All the phases of play shown in this book set (Defending and Attacking) came from an extensive video analysis of the team's matches during the 2011-2012 season.

This analysis concerns the team's function in all the four phases of the game and its aim was to show the elements which led to the huge success of Jose Mourinho's Real Madrid team.

THE ATTACKING PLAY CAN BE BROKEN UP INTO THREE STAGES:

The **first stage** includes mainly short passes from the defenders to the midfielders, although Real would often play long balls towards the forwards evading the second stage.

The **second stage** includes diagonal and vertical passes mainly by the midfielders to create a numerical superiority in the centre or on the flank. Forwards were also involved in this phase with the aim of getting into positions where the final pass can be made.

The **third stage** includes the final pass or cross to the attacking players and the final shot on goal.

THE KEY ASPECTS OF REAL MADRID'S TACTICS DURING THE ATTACKING PHASE WERE:

- **Winning the ball back immediately.** This is a part of their game that Real improved upon vastly compared to the previous season. This enabled the team to dominate the opposition in the majority of their games during the 2011-2012 season.

- Mourinho created a very effective team during the **transition phase** who were extremely efficient when counter attacking. Real are viewed by many as the best in the world during this phase.

- The creation of **superiority in numbers in the central zone,** where the players mainly used short vertical and diagonal passes.

- The Real Madrid players would **always maintain** cohesion while attacking so they were always prepared for the negative transition. This level of teamwork and communication epitomised the La Liga winners as they were never left outnumbered.

- The team would make sure not to play short passes in deep areas to **prevent losing the ball** in 'risky areas.' Where Barcelona patiently play their short passes waiting to see a weakness in the opposition, Real are far more direct and try to move the ball forward much quicker

- **Long diagonal balls** were often played directly to Ronaldo and Benzema. This tactics was extremely successful during the season and led to many goals, with the forwards finding the appropriate space to receive.

- Synchronising the movement of all the players to create a **cohesive and fluid unit.** The ease with which the Real players fulfilled their roles and responsibilities was a huge part of their success.

- **Maintaining width** with the wingers and full backs' runs. When the winger's would come inside to create superiority in numbers in the central zone, the full backs were always available out wide to receive long diagonal passes.

- **Xabi Alonso** was the most important player for Real Madrid. He dictated the rhythm of the game and helped the team move from the second to the third stage of the build up play.

- In the third stage of the build up, **Mezut Ozil** was key as he made the final passes from the central zone.

- **Di Maria and Ronaldo** were extremely good at dribbling the ball towards the centre. These runs usually ended with an assist (vertical or diagonal) towards the players who timed a run into the box.

- Real Madrid would use **high swinging crosses** from the flank. This was because many of their players were very tall and this tactic took advantage of this, creating many goals.

Mourinho used Ronaldo's positioning high up the field during the defensive phase as one of his main attacking weapons utilising his speed and power in **fast breaks.**

Of course, the technical level of the players has a lot to do with Real Madrid's success and trophies, especially that of Ronaldo. For a team to perform this well tactically, they must first have an extremely high technical level.

Jose Mourinho has obviously played the key role, as he improved on the first season by making sure to use his player's characteristics and abilities in exactly the right way to bring the best out of them. The tactics Mourinho implemented worked perfectly and Real Madrid comfortably beat one of the best club sides in history to win the La Liga title by 9 points.

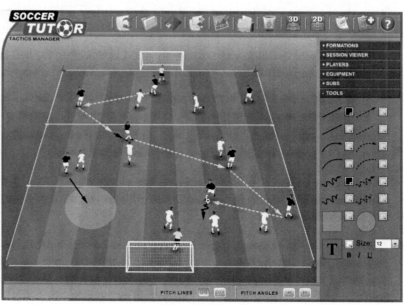

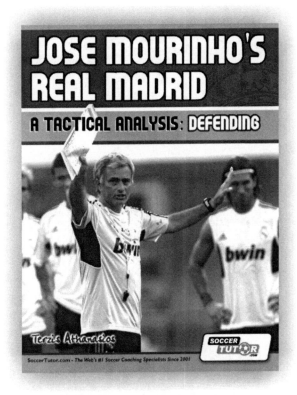

Bestselling Books

Bestselling
DVDs